The Jack of All Subtle Energies

By: **Keith Darwin Rector**

Copyright: *1996*

ISBN 0-9719673-0-X

Keith Darwin Rector

The Jack of All Subtle Energies

ISBN -0-9719673-0-X

The contract editor for this was Ellen Wood –Santa Cruz, California
Self published in USA, De Hart's printing services.
Cover by Pleasure Point Design, Santa Cruz
Distributed by Keith Darwin Rector
darwin@cruzio.com
831-479-3296

CONTENTS:

Blank

Introduction:

Our society is the most impoverished in the world when it comes to Subtle Energies. Today we are seeing the Death Knoll of scientific materialism's denial of these vast array of Subtle Energies. In it's place is a new "paradigm" of loving people and powerful advancement of spirit and soul that rivals anything in the recent history. With Quantum physics, parallel universes and many mind blowing theories with their exotic evidence, our knowledge of this world is changing fast. We can reconnect with our ancestors and access their vast knowledge to push our evolution in fantastic ways.

This book covers a vast assortment of Subtle Energy systems from all over the world that are available here today. They are transforming the way people see, feel and interact with the energy world around them. Some of these classes are wide spread (such as Reiki) while others are available only in California. Still others are evolving as you read this book today! Seek them out and Invest in your spiritual and personal evolution.

Use the tools in the last chapter to purify and cleanse the negative "Junk" that comes at us all day long in some environments. There are many out there that I have not heard of and I have "Been around " the energy world, so tell me about any you have found to be interesting. Live life the way it was meant to be lived, with access to all the wonderful energies that are around you.

Blank

Blank

6

CHAPTER ONE: SUBTLE ENERGIES AND SPIRITUALITY

This book will tremendously change your knowledge and life by changing your views. Subtle Energies are fantastic because they can make your life incredibly fulfilling and you can open up vast powers to improve yourself. Years of studying this information have convinced me that subtle energy is a necessary part of our evolution and our future. One advantage of these systems is that they require little modification of our lifestyle in order to make major accomplishments. Some of the benefits include: increasing your capacity to love and be loved, understanding how to receive love better and learning to project the energy of love in the way a lighthouse projects a beacon. Subtle Energies help us on our path of spirituality and individual advancement through lifetime changes in our own energies and their interaction with those around us. We can follow the path of our ancient ancestors utilizing all that they had available at their finger tips and so much more with the modern additional subtle energy technologies.

One power-instilling aspect of this work is the ability to take a more active participation in you own good health and well-being. Often in this sped-up world,   we feel our lives are out of control, being spent on useless consumption

and frivolous activities.   By investing in yourself with subtle energies that allows you more control over your life which helps you to find better paths, rather than drifting into negative You can actively address issues in life with the same energy used, but for positive outcome.   Too often complex medical modalities leave us   powerless to assist ourselves. However we can take command of our lives with the simplicity of these empowering energy systems.

As a parent, you will find that subtle energy is also valuable in reducing our children's pain and suffering,   again giving us an active role in helping them more. A friend once said, " When my child gets hurt   I want to 'take on the pain' so they don't have to feel it." I thought that was a true and very noble wish, but with these subtle energy systems we can reduce children's pain without ' taking it on' ourselves. That steps even further than my friends idealistic approach to reducing their child's suffering.

Subtle energies are part of a deep, rich history of ancient spiritual and healing systems used by virtually every culture on the planet. Humans everywhere use these "metaphysical" systems to achieve the all elusive "happiness" thereby pushing their spiritual evolution foreword. Most of these secrets were kept mystical and held by the core groups because of problems of people not using the energies correctly or for benefit of others. Abuse of the powers is the reason for a lot of spiritual energies being retracted by spiritual leaders in the past. Today we have much more access to information, therefore the mysteries are being cracked by tremendous advancements in science, medicine and education.

Our society has many unfulfilled spiritual needs and the price we pay shows in an unfulfilled people on a never ending search. We search in vain for a happier and healthier lifestyle, searching without realizing the source of happiness can be found in spiritual pursuits, not in the material accumulation that never satisfies us at the core level.

Many old dogmatic religions were political and not what they appeared to be. Pursuing past spiritual paths had many disadvantages, years of dedicated time combined with incredible disciplines and often "Suffering" to get further down "the path". Subtle Energy systems are usable by anyone on a spiritual path as well as the average person who wants a simpler way to reach personal goals without large sacrifices. In your life you may have already accepted responsibilities such as parenthood, home ownership, business and our lifestyle of working. It would be unreasonable for me to take five years off and travel to India or Tibet to study and apprentice in order to obtain goals. Subtle energy systems allow me and others to pursue our spiritual goals without sacrificing family life. In the Hawaiian Huna philosophy we believe that anyone can pursue their spiritual path without giving up major portions of their lives or sacrifice to convince the Creator we are worthy of attention and blessings.

Do you remember the first wave of Eastern philosophy and spiritual techniques in the 60's brought forth by Guru's and popular artists! Often this consisted of renouncing material ownership, "worshipping" teachers and masters and often with large personal sacrifices such as hours of meditation, yoga or service to others. Many I've met have searched these paths and achieved profound changes in their lives with hard work and perseverance. There are those who also searched but were disappointed when the proper blessings and "IT" did not fall into their laps with their visiting India or China (where "IT" was supposed to be.) To advance spiritually you do not have to participate the worship of personality.

These techniques were disciplines that could make a big difference in a person's life, and like many others in the counter culture we saw them as a valuable means to advance our selves. Such techniques were often more active and down-to-earth than what Christianity had offered me in the Lutheran church. Still this meant long hours of dedication and years of work, meditation and often bowing down to the religious leaders of other countries and cultures. Subtle Energy systems as taught today offer the advantages of the POWER of the eastern disciplines without the SUFFERING and SACRIFICE.

Often Western religions were very secretive about the teaching of their techniques because of a political need to keep the masses in the dark ; therefore wed us all to return often to the church leaders for guidance, rather than connecting with our higher self or ultimately Creator.

Such is the tendency of the King and Queen Monarchies where political leaders strive for an uneducated public, a populace easier to control. We of today's world have an incredible education system and access to information as compared to the past. We have the ability to make decisions based on information that is more accessible than at any point in history.

We have more power and easier physical lives than our ancestors therefore we can advance and evolve faster in our personal and spiritual lives much easily than what was allowed by leaders of the past. Yet, we have less happiness and a lower self image and self acceptance. You can change that with spiritual subtle energies.

A controlling philosophy in many religions was used so we followers would not think independently or make contact with the Creator without them. This boils down to control; Today we can reclaim our control and with guidance follow a better and more personal direction for evolution by taking control with using subtle energies.

Although our live move at tremendously accelerated speed, we are not keeping up with our lives. We can cut through the mysteries and apply these powerful subtle energy techniques to advance while speeding up our own personal and spiritual evolution at the same time. Your willingness to approach personal self-help material such as this means you are ready to move forward.

As you research the subtle energy systems available to you and ask the teachers how it has improved their own lives and you will not be disappointed in their stories. We can accelerate spiritual evolution even more with several practical systems available from all over the world with many different options never before available to the public.

Most of us now use "convenience products" that save time and effort, to save time and effort and to accommodate our still sped up world; therefore we can't take the time for spiritual advancement with the years of dedication. Our buying habits are oriented towards short cut methods for a sped up world and many do not and can not take the time for spiritual advancement. Still we need a way to make the most of our meditation time and use efficient self improvement methods. The Spiritual Unfoldment Network's classes offer much more in return for the efforts invested in our spiritual evolution.

Another beneficial aspect of these systems deals with the mental and physical health of you and your loved ones. There is little need to go into the details of how many people have health problems or how much worse off we are getting in society, so I will spare you the drama. Those who have read this far are now addressing their general health to a greater degree and the next subject will be valuable. Part of Subtle Energy systems apply to the term "laying on of hands" which means to allow a flow of energy from yourself or others with your hands, or by simply channeling energy.

It is not important for you to become a practitioner of the healing arts, but it is wonderful for you to use them only on yourself. You might never use the systems to touch another person, yet they can be a tremendous benefit to you by running the energy on yourself. This is not a technical skill like massage, polarity or acupuncture, rather a simple energy work that can be done whenever you have free time or there is nothing to do, like time you are wasting waiting for something or driving in a car or sitting in a meeting at work.

Ancient cultures knew how to cure disease by flowing life energy into a person that would balance their internal energies. Our ancestors have used the "laying on of hands" techniques for centuries until the era of "scientific materialism" came when many such things were abandoned. Now we are facing issues that western science can not conquer, by using conventional techniques against AIDS, cancer, mental illness and modified viruses. The scientific and medical industries have ignored these dedicated scientists who all along said that subtle energy and life energy existed (see my book :Life Energy Lives Again!)

In our society these mental and physical health issues have sources that can be addressed in many ways and with many modalities. What is needed are easy and yet powerful techniques that allow better health for ourselves and our loved ones, ways to reduce the imbalances and disparity within us for little investment. "Healing" can include more than physical problems such as injury or illness. Most of us have mental blocks that halt us in life's pursuits. Many people have deep hidden fears from childhood trauma and experiences that we may not be aware of.

We can work toward the root of these problems if we then move beyond the treatment of visual symptoms. A good example are the psychological issues we all carry and problems that cause what is estimated to be half of our health problems known as psychosomatic illnesses. Many of us have a hard time accepting that our minds can make us sick, we don't want to accept that we aren't perfect or that our "mentality" is ill. To even consider that our mind is not perfect is a big fear and a source of ridicule in society. Therefore, systems of spirituality can

13

enable you to be yourself and work toward your true essence without past

negative influences by energetically releasing stored negative patterns.

Few of us know or can address the powerful connection between disease

and our soul. It is important to know that with attunements or empowerments

that we are able to work on ourselves without other practitioners, or trade with

others who also practice healing and spiritual advancement.

By this time in your life you have stepped past Ego's boundaries

and have accepted that you could use a little WORK on past ISSUES.

Perhaps you are having a difficulties with a relationship or in raising children

some clues may have appeared about cleaning up personal problems

from childhood or past lives before you can move to the next set involving

children and lovers (who are also here to heal you in their own way).

Personal and spiritual evolution go hand in hand so you must peruse both.

Now that we have triggered you into thinking about all of these issues

we can address the topic of religion.

Most of today's Subtle Energy systems are very open minded as to

religious freedom. They are taught under a non-denominational system that upholds

tolerance and acceptance of many diverse backgrounds. Often, initiations are

including various religions such as Christian, Jewish, Buddhist and Taoist.

In the past, the deep esoteric information and "laying on of hands" were

reserved for the fundamental religious elitists who controlled access. In America

we associate the laying on of hands with small groups having secret or very different lifestyles that are very limiting and quite simply "boring" to us.

There is no need to conform to rigid guidelines of the past such as those

of the Shakers and the Pennsylvania Quakers.

You have the ability to embrace these systems and use them without any

religious or exoteric limits and exclusions of the past. You may also apply

Subtle Energies to the groups, Yes, of your choice and blend them with

your favorite religions. Once you look beyond isolationist religious exteriors

you will find similar goals also at the roots of their philosophy anyway! One

key to help religious (and other) bias is to look for the similarities

rather than the differences between them. We tend to look at a group or

individual with an eye for the differences first, but if we change that attitude

we will bring the world together in a more powerful way than ever.

What are we buying with these subtle energy systems ?? As consumers

we can purchase different "attunements" and ancient secret information passed

down through the ages to a select few people (found usually in fundamental religions).

We have the privilege to purchase the development and amazing blessings that

in past history would have taken years of study in a monastery or mystery school, or

perhaps be a slave to a guru or monk. This means we can advance at

a much faster rate than if we attended church or meditated as we have in the

past. Thus we have the tools to contribute to our movement on the evolutionary

path with daily meditation and activities and guidance with religious groups.

When you work or study with someone gifted with psychic abilities those abilities rub off on you or slowly transfer, like you are tuning to their radio. Such a psychic transference happens over time and is the main basis for studying under a master to achieve powerful skills. This is unnecessary to do to achieve the talents transferred down from Guru or teachers of the past. This does not mean Guru's are no longer needed, rather the old methods are being replaced, however you can still approach teachers for individual guidance for personal and spiritual growth as a matter of fact this is recommended when seeking deeper advancement.

In today's western market we can transfer the ability to tap into specific cosmic energies and to transfer that ability through a teacher to the student. This ability is similar to a radio receiver that can pick up specific radio stations or frequencies from the masses of unseen signals that are streaming through our bodies at any given time. Likewise, the radio receiver can be altered with some rewiring and the parts used as a transmitter of those stations with their frequencies as put out by the same box (or person).

If you are on a spiritual path, many of these attunements can accelerate the speed of attaining your ultimate goal without investment of time and money or traveling overseas and searching. Most teachers of these subtle energy systems are not "personality cult" types. Unlike Jones, Karesh, Moon or others, they are not into controlling you and your wallet or directing you to do their bidding. Don't be afraid to ask questions along this line, as it is a great concern to those who have heard of others mistakes about such spiritual enslavement or con games.

Most of us need to get out of our ruts that we live in and we do this by too often running straight to others people and places to find "IT". We EXTERNALIZE our needs and troubles out to something or someone else when chasing "IT", often thinking: They have it, I must have it, and I can get it from them! Maybe "It" is in their club or cult, and by joining I will be one of them. We search, but find only pieces while looking for satisfaction, often suffering many disappointments while we still do not feel complete. Loneliness drives many into dysfunctional paths, when trying to fulfill the need to belong or part of the "in crowd" (as in the gangs that pervade society today)

We need answers to our questions but we must accept that they CAN come from within. We all need to be able to contact a "Higher Intelligence" for advice and direction such as our "Higher self" or what is called the Solar angel (or guardian angel some call them). This is true contact to the inner Creator as well as to those outside our physical body.

Many worry and fret, to no end searching for answers to the questions that lay heavy on our hearts and souls. You might find that your friends are unable to help with some of those needs. Many answers can be found through learning to contact our higher self perhaps through our heart center for guidance and advice. For myself, these answers are often so simple and straight foreword that after I receive them I ask, " why was it not more obvious".

We mask and veil things in our minds with unnecessary worries, often wasting valuable time and energy.

Many Subtle Energy systems will aid you in contacting your inner resources and push your communication connecting abilities to higher levels. Start by attending an Angel workshop or class with attunements to connect with your personal Solar angel. With practice and good effort, your skill of connecting will increase tremendously. Through this method you will find the answers and guidance that you seek.

How is this done using systems from both past and present? Many have heard of Shakti or initiations given by religious and spiritual leaders that provide new found abilities for the rest of their life. Ancient mystery schools often had elaborate ceremonies and rites to empower the individual. These dramatic rituals were to insure that the individual was worthy of progressing further, and these ceremonies dedicated to the common cause or group.

Today we see remnants of these spiritual events still present in Fraternities, sororities and high social clubs. Techniques such as "hazing" were used to soften thereby allowing the spiritual energies enter. The teacher of subtle energy systems will set your brain's tuner like a radio to receive different frequencies and energies with an attunement in just a few quiet minutes. This attunement will last for life, from that point on you have access to it, and like any skill it gets better with use. Your teacher may run you (or the group) through a simple ceremony to activate the channels in you to carry the energy.

Many systems do not have and do not need a ceremony or initiation so don't expect it, different systems for different people.

In the Spiritual Unfoldment Network there two types of attunements:

1.   Activatable: This type can be consciously run on yourself or others by thinking or saying a trigger such as, "Reiki on". This type is directed down the arms, and the energy actually has "intelligence" that flows to where it is needed. These are the Laying on of hands techniques that can be run through the hands into the crown (top of head) or at specific problem locations on the body. Some systems can actually do this over a distance like a radio transmitter.

2.   Autonomous: These can't be turned on with a command or by sheer will power. They stay in the background and work when needed, like a big back pocket filled with tools that jump out when needed to do their work. Some of these open up the Nadi channels in the core of the body and channel the energies to flow. There may be others to connect with your higher self thereby facilitating better Communication, also some that can affect your past life Karma (cause and effect).

Why obtain these systems and use them regularly??

Good health costs money. In some cases you can't buy back health or purchase better health without incurring major expense. Visits to medical or psychological practitioners cost between $50 and $200 per appointment. These energy systems will in the long run, improve your health and mental well being. However they are not a substitute for medical services, but they may assist to prevent future problems.

This is a good time to mention the usual legal stuff about not being disillusioned.

19

WHEN YOU NEED MEDICAL ATTENTION, GET IT. THESE SYSTEMS
ARE A GREAT SUPPLEMENT TO THE POWERFUL WESTERN AND EASTERN
MEDICAL MIRACLES OF TODAY AND ARE NOT TO BE SUBSTITUTED!!

As a culture we Americans are spiritually starved. Past practices and
religions are out of step with the needs of today's individual, our recent ancestors
were disconnected from their spiritual background by the common misconception
of scientific materialism. These systems fill a gap in the western world and provides
the initiations and attunements lost or taken back for many years QUICKLY AND
EASILY! We have become used to convenient consumer items which allow us to continue
our busy lives without slowing us down requiring years of dedication. Subtle energy
systems spare us the time to continue life while still pursuing our right to spiritual evolution.

Increasing your self respect and self confidence is the key to a happier
life together with a healthy attitude toward all things around us. Often, this is where a
more complex subtle energy systems can really bring change to your life. Most teachers
won't talk about it because they do not want to attract those who are only interested
in this side benefit. Anyone familiar with Mantak Chia's Taoist work knows that
opening up the bodies energy channels or Nadis often increases the flow of
sexual energy for pleasure and satisfaction. You may not notice a difference
or there may only be a slight change but most people will welcome it.
Mantac Chia's work teaches you how to turn sexual energy into spiritual energy
defining a whole new spiritual power hidden in sexuality. This allows you to harness
your sexual power instead of being driven or enslaved by it.

Costs of the systems vary and your financial commitment must be considered as your individual budget dictate. At the very least, everyone should be Reiki "level one" certified, which is not very expensive as shown in that chapter. As with the cost of most material things, typically you get what you pay for. In Drisana, the various levels may add up to hundreds of dollars over a period of a year or two, but it has more power and attunements which cover vast amounts of energies that can be run. This is relatively inexpensive compared to an airline flight with a stay in a India or Tibet to pursue schooling.

I have met many who traveled to other lands 'expecting' a great transformation or spiritual encounter, only to find disappointment or coming away confused or hurt. The other end of the spectrum is for a student to invest their energy into highly celestial spiritual systems and end up 'trashed out' by trying to advance too fast for their pace in life. Many new (SUN) systems are balanced, more grounded and connected to the earth energies will keep you feeling that you can live here with your friends as you have in the past without becoming another space case. I've met many who achieve spiritual steps up the ladder, but have a hard time communicating and interacting with friends from their past. A good system will 'reach for the stars' yet keep your feet planted firmly on the earth.

Most subtle energy systems are multi-level and range from three to seven or more. The first level is often at a lower cost and will give you an idea of what the system will do for you. Then you can decide to proceed to higher levels while planning your finances and using

the time between classes to assimilate the energy. There may be a waiting

period of one month between class levels to allow the body to get

the changes integrated and higher abilities of channeling energy. In respect

the cost is spread out over time. If you work with the energies for massage, health

care or clients, you can tax expense continuing education as this can not be

received from a book.

The higher levels are stronger at accessing energy and

performing specialized functions. Teachers have various time requirements

between classes as well as prices, so do not be afraid to ask. It seems the most

polite way to ask is simply, "What is the Financial commitment".

Teachers often have free introductions or demonstrations at shows so

you can get a sample of their art. Your senses will tell you which system is

for you. You may also ask the teacher to try and contact your higher self

for suggestions on which system is the one for you.

Sensitivity and perception of an energy will vary greatly from

individual to individual. Some feel strong subtle effects of energy while others

may feel nothing at all. Feeling it is not necessary to having it work!!

You may feel no sensitivity to whoever is working on you and yet have a

powerful and profound result from it. Often, over time, your sensitivity

increases with both intent and use of your systems energies. There are several

ways that people react to having energy run on them such as deep relaxation or a perceived heat where hands are placed on them. Others may be visually kinesthetic and see colors or visual stories, while some may feel deep emotions come up and move through them.

You may also feel what other people have such as a deep Relaxation, stronger than any you have felt before. This can be a very blissful state such as Reiki land where your mind quiets down and you feel light and free within yourself. You may find that the person working on you has hands that are "hot" which produces some tingling throughout your body. Some describe it as celestial and floating up to a higher plane.

To take the classes and be empowered with a system such as Huna or Drisana can take you on a spiritual journey that over time you will feel permanent changes will occur. One description is that the heart opens up, giving the individual more capacity to love. Another reaction might be to bring up stored childhood issues that open the heart but from that comes the pain they suppressed from childhood. This may not sound like something to look forword to unless you understand the concept that you need to release this pain out of the heart in order to fill your heart with love. Moving to the other side (sometimes a far side) of the pain will be well worth the discomfort to get to your true self .

Different subtle energy systems will give different characteristics and one may be good with helping a Cancer patient while another is best for childhood trauma. Reiki for example is used by massage therapists for deep relaxation during a treatment while a more spiritual system may seem to be centered in the head or crown area. One system may be very stimulating and another more laid back and appropriate for meditation and opening the heart.

These energy systems are all working on raising our vibrational rates up and this is commonly found in spiritual paths. This means that we feel better about ourselves, live in a higher consciousness and come closer to the ideal health and vitality we were born to live with. In systems like radionics, the long term treatment goal is to raise the internal energy in a problematic part of the body to the proper frequency or "rate" of vibration. In acupuncture the same is true with the approach being to use the body energy meridians to balance and bring up the Chi energy to the proper levels.

You can actively take part in your health and spirituality with one or several of these subtle energy systems. Seek out local teachers and sample what they have available and weigh out the cost and value to your life. Consider the fact that you can work on others and be paid or barter with your abilities and see it as a return on your investment. You could use these energies in volunteering to work on local charities as a contribution and even a tax break for going somewhere nice to work as a volunteer. Costly systems may be looked at as tithing your money to the inner God/ess within just as you would contribute to worship externally in church.

CHAPTER TWO: REIKI - The universal energy for all!

Reiki is a real blessing to our society with it's simplicity and profound healing abilities. Can you imagine what the ideal world would be like if everyone were attuned to only the first level of this energy system. It would be wonderful if we could ask someone for a few minutes of soothing healing work, or to trade with them when we are tired, worried, or stressed out over life's finest moments? People with illness could have a few friends join their transmissions together to help restore balance and bring peace to their health.   Maybe one day you get off the phone with a favorite relative who has a headache, then you realize that you can help by sending them energy as a gift.

If we could all double or triple the healing energies channeled through our hands with one easy system of subtle energy, giving the potential for breaking away from heart wounds in order to realize our full emotional potential. Reiki can open up the individual's heart so the potential for loving and living will return. Think back to your childhood, find a moment when you really loved some one and remember how you felt deep in you heart. Do you recall the soft glow of warmth in the heart, the heady but pleasant high you felt for some time afterward?? When we are in this space we are actually touching our essence. With most people that feeling comes less often as we grow older and more set in the ways of society and we need to regain our hold on that space.

Dramatic events in our upbringing force us to close down many energy centers in body and mind because, socially we are not to show emotions. Traumas from our past can cause us to close away both pain and love in a dark closet, locking them away from access. With Reiki and other systems we can find the key to that closet and open up an expressiveness to allow us to find our true self. When you and follow the path in this book you are seeking your true self, and with few exceptions you will be rewarded with the treasure you find. The best thing about these methods is that we do not have to experience disaster such as the death of a loved one or great shock in life to learn to think again from the heart like a child. We can instill and rekindle the love and emotions that others conspired to take away as we evolved in our childhood.

Forms of subtle energy work have been used around the world for centuries, sometimes lost and relearned again, but always returning in response to the need's of the people. Reiki is from Japan and was brought to the United States in the 1940's, where it has been taught through a set of "Master Teachers". This system has created a wave of use by practitioners in various fields to aid in the massive undertaking of healing the world's wounds. Reiki is most often chosen by massage practitioners who use it to supplement their work by deeply relaxing both muscles and the mind. The body worker can run the energy down the arms while doing massage work or run it separately before or after. Another field that has embraced the Reiki system are nurses, another group who put their hands on people and can apply the energies freely unencumbered. Being Reiki certified at any level is a good addition to a nurse's resume.

Most of those involved in Reiki do not hire a practitioner of the Laying on of Hands work, instead, they become empowered or attuned and run the energy on themselves and loved ones. For you, a tremendous advantage will be getting together with others in exchange groups to trade Reiki with several people working on one person at a time. Group power is exponentially stronger which is how powerful medical healing was used by our ancestors in rituals.

Reiki is called the "universal" life energy because it contains a broad spectrum of frequencies that accomplish a variety of tasks. In general, the subtle energy systems have what is termed "intelligence" or knowledge of where the energy needs to go or what its purpose to do there. This strange concept involves the Angelic or Devic powers acting behind it all.

All you need to understand is that when you run the energies down your arms into another persons body, it tends to travel to the part of the body and mind that uses it best . The concept is simple, as with water , you pour energy in and it flows to the low spots until it fills to the top.

Most Reiki systems use one basic activatable energy run on a standard set of hand positions on the head, body and back, with the knees and feet optional. The higher levels use a set of "symbols" that are mostly Japanese symbol combinations to increase power and even run the energy "distant". This transmitting over a distance may not be needed by the average person, however it can be a great help when a relative or client that is a far distance and you wish to actively help them. There are several great books on the techniques but any good class and teacher will supply a book with clear instructions. Beware of teachers who offer the Reiki attunements for a low cost with little to no instructions. Ask first if the teacher has instructions or book that is included. Getting the attunements without instruction is like being given the keys to a Corvette on your 16th birthday and let loose on Laguna Seca raceway. Just getting the attunements would be recommended only if you have friends who will teach you the proper hand positions, history and ethics. However, you would still need to buy the books for additional hints and you would also not get the hands-on techniques and feedback you would in a class with an experienced teacher.

Be aware that some Reiki teachers went in slightly different directions and altered the politics. Some Reiki systems now have seven levels instead of the original levels. Some systems are very expensive, for one to achieve "Master" ($10,000) which is the third degree in most systems and then you can give others the "Power " or abilities. Others charge one tenth of that price and yet still trace their roots back directly to the originator Mrs. Takata. Is there a difference??? Yes there are changes caused by the personality of the master that can distort the energies from master to teacher. However, many Reikis are quite similar in the consistency of energy and results.

This is something to consider and inquire about when selecting a teacher. The consistency of any ritual from a mystery school or tradition handed down is in the hands of the master to keep things "original" and unchanged. Reiki rituals and symbols are a closely guarded secret and should be respected and held with reverence by the master so that distortion is kept to a minimum. If the teacher you find has pride in where they are in the lineage of masters and respects their work, they are probably a good choice.

Teachers and systems vary in the Reiki structures such as initiation styles, some teachers may change or add ceremonies, so do not carry preconceived expectations based on others experiences. The teacher should also mention the state laws (which vary considerably) and how to conform to the rules and standards. In California, it helps to become a Universal Life Minister or join a similar organization because, other than nurses and massage practitioners few people are allowed to touch 'clients'. These laws are archaic and often not enforced, but no one should challenge the law for entertainment. Consider an old Mexican curse: "May your life be filled with lawyers." Most of this sounded scary to me at first, but it is inexpensive and easy to become a ULC church Minister, you don't need knowledge or pass a test or have a congregation.

The people in the Universal Life Church are wonderful and not of the old dogmatic mainstream Christianity. Universal Life Church - Modesto California.

There are several books written specifically on Reiki that cover the history and politics better than I am able, these are listed at the end of this chapter. You may enjoy the story and relate to it well, so I will include it in brief form. Three people were keys to bringing Reiki to light and reviving subtle energy healing under the name "Usui". In Kyoto, Japan, Doctor Mikao Usui was a Christian seminary principal (or rector). He was asked by his older pupils about healing methods by Jesus Christ in using the hands, as mentioned in the Bible. Unable to answer this basic question he searched and studied the world systems for this information. In America, he achieved a doctorate in theology at the university of Chicago but still did not find the answer to that question. After studying holy writings in Sanskrit in Northern India, he returned to Japan where he discovered various symbols and formulas in Buddhist Sutras. While living in a

monastery in Kyoto, he went on what we call a "vision quest"
to the holy mountain of Kuriyama for 21 days. To alter his consciousness
and contact higher intelligence, he meditated, fasted, sang and read the suturas.

On the dawn of the 21st day he saw a shining light moved towards
him which struck his brow Chakra point on the forehead. With the intensity
of color and power Doctor Usui feared that he was going to die. At this
point the Sanskrit symbols appeared in shining gold to him. This was the
initial reception of Reiki, Dr.Usui returned to start the laying on of hands with
resulting miracles. The second Reiki Grand Master was Doctor Chijiro
Hayshi who ran a private clinic in Tokyo where he began treating people
with subtle energies.

The American connection comes in with Hawayo
Takata. Mrs. Takata was born in Hawaii in 1900 to Japanese parents
giving her access to both sides of the Pacific ocean. At about
age 35 she was widowed, with two small children and suffering from several
illnesses. She sought relief from suffering in Japan where her inner voice had
told her to go. This same voice came to her when she was on the table awaiting
surgery, telling her the operation was unnecessary. Mrs. Takata asked her
doctor about alternatives to the surgery (sound familiar?) and was advised
of Hayshi's clinic. There, she received Reiki treatments daily and
regained her health in a few months, this convinced her to
take up the trade at whatever the cost.

Astounded by the success, Mrs. Takata studied and achieved "Master" status under the guidance of Hayashi, which gave her the ability to empower others. She returned to Hawaii where she did healing work for years, she did not teach any Masters in America until past the age of seventy. Twenty two Masters were trained by her and today most teachers can proudly trace their source to Mrs. Takata on the tree of Reiki evolution.

Group work is where the real action is!! When more than one person runs energy on another subject, the power increases tremendously. Mathematically it is exponential: if two people lay on the hands at the same time it becomes the same as four people. If three people work on you at the same time then the power is the same as nine energy workers. When you get to 10 persons running energy on another person it becomes intense! It is so deeply relaxing that your muscles melt like butter. You may find the diaphragm muscles relaxing and you have to keep telling yourself to breathe, because your body wants to completely let go, into the relaxed puddle. The results can be profound using the group exchanges where each person may take from 10 to 20 minutes on the massage table to receive energy and best of all, it is often free.

Working with groups of people have been used in religion to vastly multiply thought power which will accomplish many good things for the community. An ideal view of community would be to have a group such as the early American farming town with one simple church, that is open to several denominations or shared jointly by the religions in town.

Within this a local group of people who spend a short time doing group healing and where an individual could get the love and support they need for healing themselves. Most of us have lost the community feeling with its group energy that binds people together on a basic primal level. To regain this aspect, of bonding with others in the community. We need to make a conscious effort to spend the quality time to know and assist others around us.

Often in Reiki exchange groups this tight group feeling exists, individuals can feel safe and express the tragedies and triumphs in their lives without fear of opinion or bias. In these exchanges I was impressed at how many come into the group, open up with very personal issues and are willing to express simply to illuminate their purpose in the group. Many are looking toward future changes in a positive way by bringing up a subject in their life to work on.

Realize that becoming Reiki level One and Two certified is actually low cost when you can treat each other for with group trades rather than paying a practitioner. Couples will also find getting attuned together gives them a wonderful technique for loving each other for life. When you are in intimate situations and both of you are running Reiki while holding each other, it can be very enhancing. Try going to a healing power point (such as Harbin or Esalon in California), run any energy system on each other and you may feel the intensity increase substantially.

Some people notice immediate changes when attuned to a new subtle energy system, for other students the changes may take six months to a year later. What happens for you will be personal, depending on your issues and your goals. Some will find physical and emotional healing but not as much spiritual advancement, as with other more spiritually advancing systems like Tibetan Drisana.

Subtle energy systems are often intelligent in their own way, one day you may be walking and your hands will turn on and start buzzing with energy perhaps because you need it. You may find yourself observing someone who is in pain across a room and your hands will simply turn on without asking. This may be a clue that you can make a difference to that person by offering Reiki energy to them at their time of need. This is hard to do at times, considering the social stigma around touching others, especially for men-to-men contact, so do offer Reiki, but be prepared for rejection (maybe they do not know about energy work).

I once offered someone with a physical problem in a massage class that I thought was an emotional release. The person accepted and it helped them considerably with a physical problem resulting from a motorcycle head injury sustained years before. They later asked me more about Reiki, although they had heard of it before, this was of considerable help in getting past a seizure of one entire side of their body. This was a situation where I was unsure of offering help and yet when I got past my fear of rejection, it worked out well for both of us. The experience was quite special and we shared a bonding after which was quite comfortable.

There is a lot of concern about taking on other's negative energies. Getting attunements are the best way to avoid this. There are many techniques to keep clear from absorbing negative energies, but they are not always effective (such as white light or grounding). An experienced light worker told of going to a school on Psychic healing and finding themselves and their classmates energetically taking on others problems. The key is to get attunements in energy systems and flowing out the negative junk going to the earth where it can be purified. Crystals and energy generators (such as in the chapter on tools) are good for catching and eliminating negative stuff from others such, as Mahogany Obsidian or the Purple Positive energy plate.

Find your ideal world by trying Reiki with a private session and if it helps, or turns you on, get level one certified. Proceed to level two to increase flow and improve versatility. Level three is for serious practitioners who are committed to teaching and empowering others. So get out there and enjoy it . The addresses following are for national organizations and can suggest local teachers or practitioners to try out. There are many books now on Reiki.

Blank

CHAPTER THREE: DRISANA, the Tibetan Spiritual energy.

Throughout history the Tibetans have long been known for intensely powerful and highly aspiring religion, spirituality and philosophy . Many incredible stories were brought back to Europe by travelers of highly evolved spiritual leaders and their inspiring accomplishments and knowledge. Today, this is reinforced by loyal followers of their methods of higher consciousness. One only need think of the Dali Lama and his constant pursuit of world and inner peace, and you know there are millions of minds meeting in the collective conscious toward this purpose.

Anyone with a serious spiritual pursuit will be interested in Drisana because of the many attunements to help purify, cleanse and balance the chakras, subtle bodies and the physical body. The Tibetans have had tremendous experience and retained vast knowledge along these lines; they have also blessed us with a versatile energy system. Working with energies is a master key in spiritual evolution and can cut decades from enlightenment.

Could you imagine a subtle energy system that has more versatility and variability to change you and your clients profoundly? It would have the healing ability of other systems and also combined with the ability to accelerate your spiritual evolution and the potential to enhancing future incarnations. Drisana can bring you out ahead of previous work that you have done in the past whether you are Christian , Buddhist, Jewish or any denomination or path. This is accomplished with multiple attunements in the first workshop which covers aspects of our lives on all planes. Each level has attunements that work with all seven planes, and each level works with one special plane that proceeds from the ground up. This creates a more complete, balanced and fulfilling system to work with, allows you to advance spiritually and not be "in the clouds" but remain grounded.

Drisana is one of the most powerful healing systems, and like Huna it is also a very practical spiritual connection. The Tibetan Drisana system can open up energy channels known as Nadis which carry subtle energies in your body and mind. This allows an improvement in the flow of all energy systems you now use or will learn in the future. As you advance through the levels in Drisana, you can run all your energies at a higher power settings with the Nadi strands open. Do you need more power?? Most of the time you don't need to be super powered but occasionally you may have a limited time to help someone or wish to advance faster.

This quote is from the Spiritual Unfoldment Network quarterly newsletter written by Irving Feurst.

"Each level of Drisana contains an unusually large number of empowerments, many of which have no parallel in any other system. An example is the use of "power settings", which enable you to increase the force of not just Drisana but any subtle energy system. If you have been initiated into any other energy system, you will be able to use this empowerment to run that energy stronger than you ever have before. "

"Drisana is one of only a few energy systems in the world which work with all seven planes of reality - the physical, emotional, mental, Buddhic, atmic, monadic and the cosmic. Most systems neglect the atmic and monadic. Unless we can connect deeply into all seven planes, there is some part of us which feels incomplete. "

"Drisana is the only energy system in the world that works by directly accessing the star tetrahedron shaped energy fields surrounding our six incarnation centers (also known as permanent atoms). Our physical body chakras, aura etc. are but manifestations of these fields. "

Most psychic healers use their personal energy to do the work while these systems use cosmic energies which offer a vast source of different rates and frequencies. To flow more energies this way, these energy systems open the Nadis and the strands inside them to hold and flow more energy and integrate it into our lives. The Nadis must be opened one at a time, and most people take lifetimes to open five strands. This is done with several levels of Drisana, also Huna, with time in between classes to integrate the changes.

Another concept with these energy systems is that they carry intelligence. When we run these energies they have the ability to go to where they are needed in the body and mind and to work on the problem. This amazing ability is like a computer program that has intelligence and can perform actions at blazing speed; but has no soul or life as we know it. This intelligence works further for you when you ask the energies to work on something specific. For example, you may ask Drisana to work on your headache or stomach ache and help out with that. This allows the ability to work generally or specifically on problems, and provides help in checking out the thousands of energy channels in our body and subtle bodies.

Drisana empowerments and their implications (this is only for one level of Drisana, there are several more.).

1.   AWAKENING YOUR KUNDALINI.   A powerful and completely safe method of working with Kundalini energy.

2.   ANGELIC FORCES ATTUNEMENT.   Yes, angels are real -as many Drisana graduates will testify, working with them is not only a joy, but can tremendously accelerate your spiritual evolution. This attunement facilitates communication with any angelic forces that wish to work with you.

3.   ALLEVIATION OF KARMA.   This procedure alleviates karmic burden, from the past, but does nothing to affect karma accumulated in the present life. It is guaranteed to do something for everyone, though the amount varies from one person to another. Your Drisana teacher can activate the procedure, but has no personal control over how much Karma is alleviated.

4 - 10. SEVEN ATTUNEMENTS.   This works on the seven sub planes of the

etheric plane to clear blockages in the subtle body. These attunements expand the first two strands of the nadis to hold more prana.

11.   HEART CENTER ENHANCEMENT.   Increases the ability of the heart to give and receive love at human, Devic and divine levels. Releases a healing energy from the heart, increases flow between the heart and the higher self., and prepares the heart to receive the enhancements of the higher levels of Drisana. Allows you to send heart energy into your environment without touch.

12.   ETHERIC HEART ATTUNEMENT.   This attunement works on the "Etheric Heart" (thymus gland) to open you up to acceptance of the divine will.

13.   FIRST LIGHT ATTUNEMENT.   Makes basic Drisana energy more coherent and penetrating; increases its power by a factor of five to seven. First light can effect transformation on the physical, emotional, mental and spiritual levels.

14.   SOUL / SPIRIT ATTUNEMENTS.   This series of attunements accelerates personality - soul fusion to a rate not possible in other systems.

15.   MEDITATION ATTUNEMENTS.   These increase the depth, breadth and ease of meditation.

16.   CHANNEL BUILDING ATTUNEMENT.   This increases the efficiency of channel building, a procedure to work with your central channel from your soul star to your earth star. (The soul star, an energy center of great spiritual significance, has been called the eighth Chakra by some and is located in your subtle bodies six to eight inches above your head.)

17.   SOUL STAR ATTUNEMENT.   Increases your awareness of the soul star and its significance, as well as your ability to work with it.

18.   STAR TETRAHEDRON ATTUNEMENT. For thousands of years the star tetrahedron has been recognized as one of the most important shapes in sacred geometry. Stars, planets, angels and humans (including all our chakras and our permanent atoms) are surrounded by star tetrahedron shaped energy fields. This attunement works with our naturally occurring star tetrahedron fields in an entirely new way. Once activated it passes through three phases (taking roughly 45 minutes to do so): energy work, personality integration, and personality - soul fusion. Many people, including those with extensive backgrounds in energy work, report shifts from this attunement not obtainable with any other form of work.

19.   CHAKRA RELEASE PROCEDURE. Chakra release works on one Chakra at a time to release blocked energy on the etheric, emotional and mental levels.

20.   STABILIZATION ATTUNEMENT. Using this after any procedure that affects your energy flow acts to stabilize any change that has been produced.

21.   "POWER SETTING" ATTUNEMENT.   This attunement allows you to use any energy or procedure you have at any power setting from zero to five in half unit increments. Your current power level will correspond to a setting of three after you receive this attunement. In other words, not only does this attunement allow you to "fine tune" your energy flow, but everything you already have becomes

more powerful. If you work with any new energy systems in the future, the normal

level of flow for that system will be attuned to you at level three.

22.   ACTIVATION BY WILL ALONE. Allows you to activate any energy or

procedure you have through intention alone. This applies to any energy or procedure

you now have and any you receive in the future. NO MORE HARD SYMBOLS.

23.   DRISANA ABSENTEE SYMBOL.   Empowers you to use a simple symbol

(the only symbol in first degree) to transmit Drisana energy over long distance.

24.   MODE SETTING ATTUNEMENT. Allows you to run the Drisana

energy in any one of fifteen modes: regular, stimulation, relaxation, subtle body

healing, creativity, meditation, grounding, pain reduction, balancing, clearing,

aligning, healing sleep, integration, mental alertness, or self-selecting (automatically

selects at each point in time the most appropriate of the previous setting in accord

with the higher self).

25.   TRANSDIMENSIONALITY ATTUNEMENT. Assists you in experiencing

the state of meditation in which your mind is both inside and outside of space and time.

26.   SAMADHI ATTUNEMENT.   Assists reaching of advanced states of

meditation.

27.   MENTAL CONTROL OF ENERGY ATTUNEMENT.   Increases mental

control of energy.

28.   LIGHT CARRYING CAPACITY ATTUNEMENT. Enables the physical

nervous system to absorb and integrate more spiritual level energy.

29.   MENTAL IMAGERY ATTUNEMENT.   Increases ability to work with

mental imagery.

30.   SEVENTH RAY INITIATION.   The seven rays of creation are the most significant of all energies. Just as all substances are made up of some combination of the elements, all subtle energies are made up of some combination of the rays. Each level of Drisana has an initiation for improving the ability of your chakras to absorb and work with the energies of one of the rays. Beginning the last day of Drisana one, and continuing for seven days, you will feel beautiful seventh ray energy streaming into your crown, spreading throughout your body and permanently transforming your chakras.

There is also another subtle energy system called Neriya (ner- ee - ya) that is stronger at pushing your spiritual evolution but requires that you take three levels of Drisana before taking the first level of Neriya.   It is described as a spiritual warrior energy for the person who wants to advance faster and is willing to put up with more pushing. You need the three levels of Drisana to be able to handle and hold the higher energies of Neriya. It is a more expensive and intense system, but worth it for faster advancement if that is your wish.

Drisana is a life-long set of permanent attunements enhance your subtle bodies and the way they absorb or transmit energies. To understand more we will examine the theories put forth by Irving Feurst, Alice Bailey and other teachers. The sources of these energies are through what are called "planes" There are seven basic planes of existence. These are not to be seen as a physical location such as New York or your back yard, rather they are to be seen as existing in the same place. Like a ladder there are steps up and a process to reach each step you must learn like taking the first steps in life as a child does. The first three are physical and fairly obvious, the physical, mental and emotional. Our house and car are very physical, our thoughts are things on the mental plane and emotions and their results are on an emotional plane.

In the middle is the Buddhic plane and which is like a person standing on the border between two countries over the line. One-half is in the physical plane, the other half is in the spiritual plane or a border zone. Many energy systems draw their energy from the Buddhic plane which is easier for most of us to access. The upper three planes are spiritual and many who have gone there in their minds describe "mystical experiences". These planes are the Atmic, Monadic and Cosmic layers above the physical and reach up higher in vibrational rates towards our concept of God/ess.

The Buddhic plane is the plane of spiritual union where the love aspect is mediated through the mental plane. Most of the energies available today draw from the buddhic plane like Reiki and others. There is more information on the highly technical specialty can be found in the Alice Bailey books and several interpretations of these texts that may be more appropriate.

Drisana and other systems reach into and through all seven planes to advance and push our spiritual evolution. The energies that we run from our hands are single or combinations of what are termed "Rays". Mystery schools often refer to 3, 7, or 12 rays, depending on the teacher.

For example, the three primary rays can be combined or mixed with proportions to form the next four rays, with a total of seven rays (most referred to). They, in turn, can be combined or mixed to form five more rays with a total of 12 rays. There is a 12 ray system taught in the Spiritual Unfoldment Network that enhances any other subtle energy systems you may have learned and this can greatly increase the power to channel energies.

Each of the rays has polarity characteristics of Yin or Yang, that are analog (variable content) in between. This is like a train that goes through 12 towns, but you can leave the station at each town and travel north or south from each particular town. All subtle energies come from a mix of these 12 rays. Drisana and Neriya have a broad range and variations of the primary rays.

The keys to spiritual advancement are meditation, channel building, and running various energies that can purify, cleanse and balance yourself. It is up to you to discipline yourself to do these on a daily basis. Some have a difficult time with this and are more group-oriented, so if you look for a church or ashram to work with others in a common interest.

There are seven levels of Drisana , each one dealing with different planes and their energy has higher level specialties. The results will be particular to you and you will have to balance the costs and benefits with your abilities. The first level of Drisana has 30 Attunements in it and the second has 40. This a lot to work with but can really push your spiritual advancement.

Contact:
        Spiritual Unfoldment Network
        Irving Feurst
        P.O. Box 5900
        Hercules, CA
        www.spiritunfold.com

        Or Keith Rector
        darwin@cruzio.com
        http://www.spiritunfoldment.com

USES:

Drisana can help balance, clear and align the Chakra's and meridians.

It can also be used for working on issues from childhood and past lives.

You can bring up vibrational rates of organs and nervous systems.

To get the full benefit of the energies, use them daily for a few minutes

(after meditation for example).

Relaxation, stimulation, deepen meditation and many others.

Blank

CHAPTER FOUR: HUNA, the Hawaiian Traditional Energy.

The Kahuna of Hawaii kept their secrets hidden from the
western world.   The Huna or "Secret" is out now and you can learn and use the
ancient systems preserved by the Hawaiian ancestors. If you are seeking a
down to earth, heart centered spiritual system to keep you balanced then
Huna is your calling. Huna is a wonderful spiritual and healing system that
has been brought out of hiding and is available here on the mainland USA.
Huna is a major world spiritual tradition and gives us a call to the heart.

Ancient isolated cultures are, perhaps, the best record of uncorrupted religion
in the world. Hawaii was just such a place, their spiritual systems uncorrupted
in the middle of the Pacific for most of existent when the western sailors appeared.
Such concealed cultures were often forced to keep their deepest religion and mysteries
well securely hidden after the western settlers came with the intent to "civilize them".
For centuries Hawaiians held a wonderful mystical and spiritual system with
the information passed down through many generations verbally, and through dance.
The Christian missionaries, in their rampant desire to rub out the old religions,
simply ignored and suppressed the Hawaiian native religion and spirituality. This is

truly a mistake for the missionaries could have learned vast amounts of loving caring methods from one of the oldest most pure religions on the planet.

This fact came to light in the 1900's through the writings of a famous westerner with an open mind named Max Freedom Long. Good old Max found the deeply religious techniques and wisdom already used for centuries by the Hawaiians also present in many of the worlds religions. The Huna system had more of them in one system, therefore, had a complete religion / psychology / philosophy path, more than most on our planet.

Max's understanding of this knowledge is best seen in his book : "Huna Code in Religion", where correlation's with other religions are revealed. The book examines the similarities in various religions and does not dwell on their differences, as most of us and the leaders do. Max Freedom Long looks into the deep hidden meanings in other writings from around the world. Max cracked the secret code in the Hawaiian language, which was an oral and dance tradition of passing on the secrets. For example, the word "Hawaii" can mean supreme breath by the water, while today we may see it as supreme breath work by the water. There can be several meanings for each word or component in the Hawaiian language. Hidden meanings are always present, and the esoteric content is remarkable.

Today, several groups teach the work of the Hawaiian Kahuna and their ancient secrets from Max Long or others who actively follow the Huna philosophy. Some are held in Hawaii and others on the mainland

and in the mid west there is an organization on Huna research. One is advertised on the Internet (under Huna) and Serge King is well known in Hawaii. A few groups of teachers on the mainland are doing advanced Huna work, one is run by Irving Feurst (SUN) and the other is Laura Yardley, both are in California. Realize that Huna is a major world spiritual tradition, as powerful as others, but less known.

The Huna system taught by the SUN network follows the Malaka tradition and, like Drisana, has several attunements with each level. The Hawaiian Huna system of energy work is both a form of laying on of hands and a spiritual path, and comes with a very reasonable price. The source is from the ancient Polynesian systems found at the root of the Hawaiian culture, there are parallels to many South Pacific island paths of religion. One of the BEST parts of Huna is the belief that everyone should pursue the paths of spirituality, not only an elite core of the privileged few. Which is a very practical way of addressing the issue as many find a dead end with other religions, unless they choose to devote their entire life to follow a restricted lifestyle.

If you have visited Hawaii, you certainly know that the subtle energy found there is heart oriented and cherished by romantic vacationers and honeymooners. It is claimed that Hawaii is the heart chakra of the world. Huna is both open-hearted and open-minded. The Hawaiian Kahuna were open to other beliefs and the SUN teachers agree that all knowledge does not come from one source. Be open to studying other religions, examine esoteric traditions from around the world to get a complete picture of life.

Quoting from the SUN network quarterly newsletter by Irving Feurst: "Known as HUNA (meaning "secret"), the Hawaiian spiritual tradition places equal emphasis on connecting with your spirituality and connecting with the earth, your body, and your emotions. Rather than teaching transcendence of the physical plane, HUNA teaches us to celebrate life, to merge matter and spirit."

"The HUNA philosophy believes that the key to living a fulfilled life lies in the awakening and integration of your subconscious self, conscious self, and higher self. It offers us a profound beautiful philosophy of life centered in love and the vision of humankind, nature, and the divine as harmonious parts of a cosmic community. But Huna is not just a philosophy; more than anything else Huna is something you do! It gives us a set of practices that are simple yet, when used regularly, profoundly transformational. To bring in energy, direct it, and integrate it is a key to spiritual advancement. "

The SUN network teaches a sequence of classes called "Huna ."
The ancient Hawaiians used the word Kahuna (literally "keeper of the secret") to refer to a practitioner of Huna and here we use the word "healing" in the full sense of "making whole". (The English words "heal" and "whole" come from the same old English root). Like all SUN classes, Kahuna Healing is an initiation workshop in which you receive powerful attunements that you can then access at any time, for yourself or others, by mentally directing the flow (no visualization, mantras, etc.). The workshop leader is trained in the Malaka tradition of Huna. The teacher

transmits directly to the student, through permanent empowerments of the student's energy field, abilities which would otherwise take decades to develop. This is called "Shakti" in India and "Empowerments" in Buddhism.

To help understand the inner workings of the Kahuna knowledge you should have a taste of the structures of the system and relate it to western psychology and philosophy. The Hawaiian's viewed people as consisting of three parts that make up the individuals being. The lower self (Unihipili) or what we discovered centuries later as the subconscious which is located in the solar plexus and body. This special part is not apparent to our thinking mind, but stores our life's events and powers. Our ability to store life energies or forms of "CHI" are contained there, as well as separate "minds" such as the abdominal brain and the Heart where many people listen for information. The Institute of Heartmath in Santa Cruz, California works with the mind of the heart and teaches people to communicate with this vast part of the lower self and look inward for answers about ourselves.

The second part that we most often get stuck in all too often is the conscious (Uhane) or middle self. This is our daily mind, in our head, that gets us through our daily lives that most of us relate to. This part of us is often disconnected from the lower self. Many have conflicts between these two selves which can cause extensive problems both mental and psychosomatic illnesses. Interaction between our lower and higher self is revealed in our dreams and desires, they can be accessed by hypnosis so we may find answers to these conflicts. The Hawaiian Kahunas used many methods and had more knowledge about complex psychology than ever experienced by western medicine.

The top of the chain is the higher self (Aumakua) or the superconscious which is the connection to the higher beings such as the Creator and Angels. The Hawaiians refer to the higher self as "older utterly trustworthy" parental spirit or "guide". In the Spiritual Unfoldment Network it is referred to as the Solar Angel and is an intersection of your soul and the guardian angel just above your head (Some call it the Eighth Chakra). This is where most of western science and belief stops short. The Higher self has divine qualities such as patience, love and compassion. When the three selves are out of alignment they can cause disease and emotional upset. In Huna, the goal in life is seen as awakening and being in touch with the three selves. When our three selves are aligned and in harmony this is conductive to happiness. I have found this to be true.

Getting the three selves to communicate and work harmoniously is the key to getting things together in the spiritual world, which is why Huna is a very balanced system to learn. There is an emphasis on being grounded and being present in the heart, as well as reaching for the cosmic light to expand our spiritual evolution. The miracle producing abilities of the Kahunas are achieved by using Mana or life energy sent up from the lower to the higher self while using a deep breathing prayer technique. The details are covered in several good books at the end of the chapter. This is called the "HA RITE" and is taught in the Spiritual Unfoldment network Huna 1 workshop.

Conflicts between the conscious and unconscious selves are today recognized as repressed emotions. Psychosomatic illness is another term used but Hawaiians have known about this hidden issue for hundreds of years before Freud chomped his first cigar. Methods in Huna actually dissolve emotional conflict at the unconscious level without having to experience the problem or issue and having it come to the surface. This is a profound tool for the hypnotherapist, who normally has their patient relive the experience and then empower themselves.

The Hawaiian description of Mana, or life force, is much like water in that it fills, then rises to wherever it is needed. Use of the Mana was done with the HA Rite and can be used by anyone once you have learned the technique whether you have had attunements or not. Several large groups that teach Huna techniques, others that give initiations or Shaktis to empower people for life with new abilities and strengths. In the Spiritual Unfoldment Network, the Malaka tradition is taught with seven levels of achievement, the first level teaches the Ha Rite.

Many talk about getting too cosmic or getting spaced out on spirituality. Some students end up with their heads in the clouds and can not relate to normal daily life. Huna emphasizes reconnecting with the earth and to balance both grounding and spiritual advancement.

This blending of spirit and material things is the cornerstone of Huna.

It is an advantage to many who are often stuck in their heads

float around in an emotional turmoil or go through old loops to

review negative past experiences.

Huna can teach you many techniques to combine with meditation Similar to the micro cosmic orbit of Tantric (and Mantac Chia's work) it can also enhance the meditation effects. The Huna orbit circulates energy within the body, but passes the loop through the heart twice per cycle, giving a more heart-oriented approach. In the higher levels of Huna a technique for meditation uses a method similar to the tree of life in the Jewish mystical.

Using Huna combined with other systems like Reiki or Lovestream can greatly enhance your work. The higher classes of SUN network Huna give you an attunement for the universal combining of several energies at once. This means you can run Reiki and Huna out of your hands at the same time with powerful results. There are thousands of energies out there and you can blend many together to achieve tremendous results. These are intelligent energies that are like a divine computer program and are made to work on many energy channels and aspects of healing.

Huna is also very dream oriented. There are attunements for dream recognition and recalling to assist you in your dream work. (even one to charge water). Energy work is the heart of Huna which includes a broader spectrum than most energy systems available to the public. These aspects make a complete and versatile energy system available in Huna.

Many spiritual traditions throughout the world speak of transcendence of the physical plane. Many try to transcend the physical plane for a while but at some point they must come back and do the dishes. Huna says this is not true, you are born with a body and must return to it and live with the rest of us. If you find the most spiritual person on the planet, they are still in a body. Huna says that you will be in that body until you die, therefore you might as well enjoy the trip. There is emphasis in Huna on pleasure and enjoying life. Therefore it is grounding and heart oriented to keep our feet on the ground and not let our heads get too high in the clouds.

This is also reflected in the deep connection to nature and mother earth. Many problems emerge from loosing contact with the earth. Nature is very healing but we isolate ourselves from the earth in the ways we live. One example is that spiritual teachers will refer to a major problem and shift in humanity from the invention of shoes. This may not seem like much, but it has a profound impact in our grounding with the earth. You must keep your feet on the earth to reach to the sky.

Our shoes isolate us from contacting the earth and it's energies. This is shown when people are too much in their heads and with too much energy in the upper Chakras which keeps us out of balance. How many do you know that fit that description, and how does it affect them? Does it leave them scattered and wobbly at times, overcome with emotions and worries. Why is it so important to not be stuck in your head all the time?? Perhaps we have a need to ground

in this culture but we have never been taught how, other than to plant a garden!

With advanced Huna techniques we connect with mother earth more easily

by using a broad spectrum of frequencies. You can also transmit healing energy to the

earth when you are in nature. Another technique is the cross of fire meditation that

uses points common with the Jewish tradition). There are few parallel

energy systems with that kind of work.

The Spiritual Unfoldment Network's first level of Kahuna healing

includes the following attunements:

Subconscious cleansing - Clear out trauma's without bringing the up consciously

Mental clearing - Shake out the minds cobwebs.

Healing energy - to make whole spiritually

Cross of fire meditation

Harmonizing the three selves. - Get the Lower, Middle and Higher Selves to work

together harmoniously

Books: Max Freedom Long
Secret Science behind the Miracles.
Huna Code in Religion

HUNA Research Inc. Teach Huna Techniques, may not do attunements.
1760 Anna ST.
Cape Girardeau, MO 63701
314 334-3478

Books:
Heart of Huna by Laura Yardley
P.O. Box 40
Mill Valley. CA 94942

Spiritual Unfoldment Network.

Serge Kali King
He is on the net under Huna
Hawaii.
Quest books
P.O. Box 270
Wheaton, IL. 60189

Non Huna but heart oriented.
IHM Boulder Creek CA. (Books, workshops, designer music that is great.)
Planetary publications.
P.O. Box 66
Boulder Creek, California 95006

Blank

CHAPTER FIVE: ANGELS are Here and Clear.

Angels are our bio-computer network to the cosmic world and you can connect to incredible guides and helpers by learning to link up. There are wonderful cosmic energies to be found if you can open up your mind and receive help through these incredible blessings. Our ancestors had been more connected with, and interacted with the higher self and the Angels, also they were more in contact with nature and spirits before they were taken over by "civilization".

Few have a good definition of what angels are, or what they can do for our lives and spiritual pursuit. For centuries we have been separated and pulled away from them, but now is THE time to reconnect for many benefits. Today there is a big interest in Angels and what they are telling us, and sales of Angel products being sold for millions of dollars, to remind us on a daily basis of their presence among us. Here you will find some of their purpose in your life and if that pleases you, then definitely do pursue the references shown and classes.

Angels are spiritual beings that are on a separate yet parallel evolutionary path beside ours. They are complementary to humans and we can help with each others evolution. They benefit from our relationship in that they are in a process of descending down through the planes while we are moving up. I refer to the guardian angel as a solar angel in a general term because guarding over us is only part of their job. It is of mutual benefit to work with Angels and it can be vastly rewarding.

Angels have a definite purpose, they help us follow a spiritual and personal evolutionary path. They also have side purposes that are well known to people who have encountered them such as the role of being a "Guardian Angel" that watches over us, warns and prevents major disaster. There are many stories about people being helped by a "stranger" with whom they felt total trust in, but when they looked back the helper has disappeared. To some, Angels appear in their full Etheric winged form to bring news or guidance. If you have not encountered yours, then maybe you are following the path and there is no need for them to interfere or interact with your life, so don't sweat it!

Angels are not "dead people with wings and lots of time on their hands," rather they are bodiless beings on a parallel path and trying to both help and also learn from us. They are on a higher plane, learning to descend or condensing to our level and we are on a lower plane trying to move up towards their world. Through interaction we improve our lives while improving theirs in group advancement and cooperation, and this is an evolution of the future. They are dual to us and we to them, and we are moving toward a point in between where we someday hope to meet.

We have a wonderful advantage on Earth in that we have "free will" and can choose our path without interference. Angels have respect for this freedom and, therefore, will not "bust" us for acting stupid nor treat us like children, rather they work with us.   Most of us are aware of the presence of our own personal Angel by the inner voice called intuition. One type of Angel is assigned to us for our life, which is our solar or guardian Angel and they act as an interface to the Creator and the higher Angelic kingdom.   Just as we have specialists in our culture, so there are other Angels that have specialized purposes to perform.

The "higher self" is a term commonly used in Spirituality like the Huna system which means a blend of our soul and the Guardian angel working together for spiritual advancement. This is often shown as an eighth chakra above the head, which looks like a number eight on its side, or like an infinity symbol floating about one foot above (Tarot cards). You can train yourself to communicate with your solar angel and ask for help or guidance, then actually ask questions and receive "yes" or "no" answers and later full instructions. To most, this seems bizarre only because we've never been taught how to do it. Think about the apprehension you felt the first time you encountered a video game or computer and how little of those emotions and fears were even valid.

Angels can be more than simply a guide or physical helper. In an emergency they can bring about physical manifestation with powerful results.

Angels overlook entire countries and states as well as support spiritual business and football Angles must be gnarly! Many books (including Koran, Tora and the Bible) tell stories of their great deeds and there are sightings by large groups who have seen the same vision of Angels even on battlefields and other startling places.

In some encounters that the Angel does not appear as anything other than another person who has the answer that we need or provides the tool or skill to fix an immediate problem. These are commonly experienced when you are in trouble and suddenly someone appears out of nowhere to help, and then disappears into thin air. It is common to see or project an image of someone whom that person respects or believes in a mentor from the past. This type of projection of a certain superficial image from the mind is beneficial for faith in the help offered from the Angel. Other sightings are truly an intense experience in an emergency or critical time when the individual is definitely at the end of their rope or they need a dramatic change in life to survive.

Many ask " If angels are available to us at all times, why do they let so many suffer on this overstressed planet, and why can't we connect more easily." Their job is not to interfere with or change our suffering or struggling but to respect our free will. Buddhists know that most of our suffering is created in our minds and can be stopped there. For example, world hunger could end if not for people's politics. There are various reasons that we have been disconnected from the Angels which I'll discuss next, but the key thing is that we can reconnect and benefit tremendously from such a reunion.

The Christian religion that most of us were raised with went through a period of emerging from other religions, actually it evolved during early Roman times which affects us today. Edgar Caycee spoke about how the early bible was more extensive, and was then edited by Constantinople and other religious leaders. Sanskrit bible transcripts (recently made public after forty years) have supported Caycee's historical anthology. Politically, church leaders had dropped the reincarnation philosophy for the Heaven / Hell rules, which meant a more exoteric trend in church leadership. Leaders wanted the public to access the Creator through them rather than develop abilities to communicate directly with the Angels.

Church leaders wanted to have exclusive access to the Angelic kingdom. After all, if we knew how to access the Angels ourselves why would we need such leaders for?? Ancient cultures such as the Hawaiians rely on the Solar Angel for daily guidance and regard them as a normal part of their makeup. There has been a thinning of the "Veil" and people have become more open to the Angels consider the popularity of books and statues with Angels. Many people around the world are connecting and learning about the huge network available to us if we make the effort and reach out to this forgotten part of our psyche. Do you want to connect more with angels, working with angels can vary in many ways. You may have trouble tuning in, and it can take months or years, but with patience you will find it very rewarding.

Psychologically, there is much resistance to Angels and being able to connect with them and have confidence to get results. Often we have blocks or fears that prevent us from getting our requests through and wishes fulfilled. One book that should be first on your list if Angels are interesting to you is " Ask Your Angels." We all have conscious and unconscious blocks, and resistance to authority figures from the past upbringing by parents, teachers and mentors that we had bad experiences with. This colors our view of an authority figure such as angels or the religious leaders as well, also we project those fears and judgment onto them incorrectly. It is extremely hard to turn off bias, more so when you can't physically meet these etheric beings.

The first thing recommendation for contacting your solar Angel is to ground, and the second is to release any fear, judgment or resistance to your request or fear of receiving help from the Angelic network. Most have fears of receiving something that will change their lives and make us adapt to a new path. There may be unconscious guilt about not being worthy of receiving something. Many will need regular practice to get past these blocks; some will drop out without trying if they get little or no results, so do not have unrealistic expectations! Start with simple things to ask or receive. None of this, "Oh lord, won't you buy me a Mercedes Benz..."

Many people fear that connecting with the creator or believe that it is sinful to approach the creator without divine help. Others will not try, fearful that the vengeful, wrathful, angry God will punish them with lightning, or worse. Ben Franklin was condemned by church members when he played with a kite and key during a lightning storm to prove electrical activity. The clergy felt that lightning was God's punishment, and not man's to play with. We would still be using candles and wood fires if that belief had stopped inventors like Ben Franklin.

Many good books and classes are available to teach you how to connect with the Angel that will be your buddy. The SUN teachers have several classes with attunements that improve communication and run Angel energies. They are low cost ($40) and take a half day to receive attunements and instruction. Meditation attunements are included in some classes to take home and use daily and work well with techniques taught in "Ask Your Angels" such as the mantra "EE NU RA." Both books and general classes without attunements can improve your connection to the higher self with active methods and meditations, however attunements do help. Some books are only accounts of peoples encounters while others give techniques and meditations. Books on encounters you may want to request from the local library while others like "Ask Your Angels" you may wish to own as a reference guide. "Angels Within Us" by Randolph Price is another.

The kind of things you may want help with can vary, so don't be afraid to ask trivial questions for practice and extending your connectedness. I often ask stupid things like " Are there any good things for me at the Goodwill store today?" Or " should I even stop at the store today??" You may ask help by requesting that your higher self interact with other people's Angels to help some healing.

Hawaiians and many ancient cultures believed that all higher selves can communicate. This is similar to putting the word out on the computer network to assist you in a working with others and giving new direction where before there was none. This is an Internet access beyond comprehension.

After asking questions, some will receive words or full sentences, but most of us may get sensations of energies that indicate a yes or no answer. Depending on your kinesthetics you may not feel energies but may receive information by visual or other inputs to your senses. This varies considerably from person to person. There may be no answer at all and that could be a neutral answer, or you are not connected and grounded enough to communicate. This may also indicate that it can't be answered at this time. You should always consider there is a third possibility that needs further questions, or another event to occur before a solid answer can be reached. Have patience with the work and it will reward you well although it may take months or years of intent.

There is a hierarchy to the angelic world and the structure has been discussed in several books that vary with their belief system. Often many connect up with their higher self and come to believe they are in contact with higher level Angels such as Michael or Gabriel. This may not be so, rather their own higher self allows them to project that image in a way of achieving respect. Some who channel bring information from their guardian Angel, thinking it is an Archangel. This is one of the classic problems in metaphysics. The information may be valuable, but not clear or concise.

The Angels are a highly structured system with a hierarchy that is tiered or leveled which steps up like a pyramid with the creator at the top. The highest offices are held by the Archangels that govern or cover all locations, not only the earth. They have tremendous responsibility and rarely interact with usual humans but work through the lower angels that are more intimately in contact with us. When you work with your solar Angel you can access many types of other Angels for help and guidance, but it is rare to need access to the highest level of the angelic kingdom. There are a classical 22 Angels that work with the earth to further our evolution and progress. (Angels Within Us)

There may be several angels that you work with as you advance through spiritual systems such as Drisana or Neriya where you are matched up with an Angel to help you work on yourself. The Angel workshops offered through the Spiritual Unfoldment Network help you to get aquatinted with some of them.

There are many channels of information that are in contact with their higher self. The information may be valuable, but some may be hazy or distorted. This is the classical metaphysical pitfall so you must take time to be sure and understand the answers, both from others and your own questions. Do not base you life on this as many in the past have made mistakes from listening to channeled information that lead them down the wrong path.

But Don't let this detour you from goals though. Request the really big stuff through your higher self addressed to others like the solar logo's, Creator, Jesus Christ, Buddha, Allah, and others important to your belief system. Work with your Solar angel and don't worry about jumping into the mind set that "I must work with archangel Michael or Gabriel". Your solar angel can do tremendous things for you and others.

The Spiritual Unfoldment Network offers several Angel classes, one called The Guardian Angel workshop and the Angel of Unconditional Love and Freedom. There is an Angel of Creative wisdom class and the Angel of Power and Integrity (working on the Ego). A new series of Angelic opening and shielding of the heart, brow chakras is available now. Also, there is a 12 class series with Irving Feurst only, that was taught in the past with attunements for Angel energies, a great set.

Many offer classes on connecting up to the Angels. Try to get ones that have attunements and you may progress much faster.

Books:
Angels Within Us.
Ask Your Angel

CHAPTER SIX: AMANAE, for the Child's Sake

Amanae is a trip through the spiritual spin cycle.   Those who choose

Amanae are accelerating both their personal and spiritual evolution with a

powerful multi-faceted therapy that has a spiritual twist. Approach this only if

you are dedicated to powerful cleansing and the filling of light.   If you have

connected with your inner child, then you know the importance of clearing

up issues on that subject.

When we are physically or mentally hurt we feel a threat to our very life! Do

you remember a pain or hurt that caused you to contract your muscles and pull

away from the threat to protect yourself? When this happens repeatedly

we "chronically" contract with a reaction that locks into our cells and tissues in a

process called "Armoring".   Your fear from that threat can unfold

as anger. If we are not allowed to, or can't release this anger, it's bottled up

within us, then nature turns it against us. There are a handful of powerful

modalities that can reverse this by energetically releasing this mass storage of

traumas and fears.   Armoring can be released and the result is that

you become more of your true self, the self you were meant to be before others who raised you twisted your emotions permanently. A most powerful way is to take an Amanae workshop from two to five days.

Traumas from childhood are stored in the tissues of the body as well as the mind, even perceived ones that are no real threat or can cause no harm. As children we may feel that our parent or mentors do not love us or are not concerned with our well being caused from incidents that had little to do with love. Pain and suffering caused by injuries and physical damage are also locked into the cells.

Your body is like a file cabinet or a computer hard disk drive that stores and archives your life's miseries. We carry this throughout our lives like dents and scratches on a car's body as it ages. Would you like to cleanse and purify those stored cellular memories in a relatively short period of time? Do you have the desire to advance spiritually by breaking the Ebaneeser Scrooge like chains that hold your spirit to this earth. Are you willing to sacrifice a little to become "Lighter" in your spiritual evolution and shake off burdens of the past? If you are willing to go beyond the typical slower healing techniques to break the barriers , then Amanae is to be considered.

Amanae is like taking your soul out to be laundered, cleansing it, beaten on the rocks by the stream, run it through the rollers, shaken –not stirred, then hung out in the sun light to dry. When you have pumped out the negative programming forced on you by those who raised you. Then Amanae energy can take it's place. This process of emptying and filling with spiritual light is done repeatedly during a session or workshop by stripping the armor and cleansing your soul.

This is not for the faint of heart. Your commitment must be strong with the willingness to change deeply, as in the joke: "How many transpersonal therapists are needed to change a light bulb?? Only one, but the light bulb must wish to changed. " Amanae bodywork can involve experiencing the very trauma's that are stored, but with the advantage of YOUR being an adult that can regain the power lost to others as a child or from past lives. Afterward, you may experience emotions and learn to live with them in a positive way that was not allowed, when you were growing up. Quotes from those who attended the five day workshops included things: "My body was changing for weeks afterwards." " Incredible lightness." "It was the toughest thing I ever did in my life, but the best thing I ever did in my life!!" Add to this some of the most powerful spiritual energy coming in and you have a concept of this intensity.

Amanae is at least four different techniques combined to form a powerful releasing system. The practitioner does a deep tissue massage to break up the armoring or blocks, and at the same time does a deep breathing. The client on the table also does a deep breathing which helps reduce the discomfort by bringing in LIFE energy to the point of being worked on like breath work. The practitioner will stop and do a "laying on of hands" causing a flow of strong celestial energy when the client starts releasing stored negative events from the cells. This deep breathing by the practitioner stores up Prana or Mana (life energy) and is used to help transform the negative energies and release them to the earth or outward. The releasing will differ from one person to another but often includes crying, releasing anger and screaming as the traumas come foreword and are released from the body cells. THIS CAN BE THE MOST PROFOUND ENERGY WORK YOU MAY EVER EXPERIENCE.

The founder's history is a story of crisis and recovery, plus discovery of true life dedication to the work involved in helping others clear negative patterns. Christine Day was dying of Lupus in an Australian hospital and was recalling grim memories of childhood when she realized her death wish. Seeing this inner rejection of life gave her the light to see that her recovery was dependent on taking responsibility for her own healing and health. Christine's choice to live and rid herself of life-long negative patterns brought her into healing modalities involving meditation, herbal remedies and body work.

During a morning meditation, Christine received the transmission that showed her a series of cellular repatterning techniques which heal the inner child's problems and effectively breaks down armoring. These were used with remarkable results on those who came to get help from her. Next, she was directed to teach and bring the remarkable system on the west coast of America. Here in Northern California she settled down to one of the nations hot beds of radical and powerful therapies which draw many from around the world. The best quote from Chistine is "I have been given the gift of remembrance - of connecting with ALL THAT IS and living in their divine essence."

In Ukiah, California a group of dedicated individuals has formed as a team to teach and train practitioners of Amanae. Classes are often held there and also at other communities, depending on the demand. They offer both two day and five day workshops of the Amanae work where one can work with others to break through lifelong issues. They also teach a lightbody system and each year more practitioners are being made available in areas all over the state, so contact the office for literature as to finding the closest practicioner to work on your issues.

It is hard to verbalize what your individual reaction or end results might be, or what will change in your life. To define your true self at the end of five days is difficult, because it may mean big changes after months for the better that you can not conceive of yet. I can relate my personal experiences to give you an example of results and there are interviews of others who have done the practitioner training.

My attraction to Amanae was to improve spiritual development and work on my childhood traumas through cleansing and purification. What I encountered was my inner child at five to seven years of age when I lived with trauma such as abuse from my father, and from teachers in the school system. I again experienced, these traumas but played them out with different endings where I reclaimed my power and fought back the aggression to empower my inner child. I didn't have a very abusive childhood but there were experiences etched on my mind and body that had gained control of how I would react at any given time to stressful or awkward situations.

I remembered a horrible first grade school teacher who would shame us into conformity. She was a hostile, abusive dictator, which was all I could remember. But working on the heart area in a five day Amanae workshop, what came out was the hatred for the women school teachers that dominated my life for five years. I did not realize it's importance until I released this traumatic part of my life during the session, when I fantasized about bulldozing and burning down the school with the teachers inside. This was followed by a fantasy about digging up their bones and desecrating them for 1000 years. After energetically releasing this area in my heart I began to laugh uproariously at the destruction of the school and it's teachers, which is not at all like my personality. How did this change me? My attitude towards women had been tainted by these heart-felt injuries all my life without my knowledge. It has been stored in my subconscious and did not come to the surface until this work.

What this accomplished was to change the foundation of my emotions toward the women in my life. My expression of love was different, and my unconscious fear and distrust of women had changed for the better. This is one example of a released trauma engrained so young that I either did not want to remember it, or had blocked it out. I suffered abusive times from my father that came up when the lung area was worked on.

The fear of the father had impacted me in the throat and lung area from one incident, and when that came out it was clear that I was able to access much more inner power. This was a truly empowering time for me to experience the trauma, then regain control of the situation.

I was worked for over an hour on the lung area by three people, and it was tough to get through, but when I got off of the table I felt as if someone had shoveled a pile of rocks from my chest. When I stood up and walked from the room, I felt a sense of true power that was new to me, and I know it was a dramatic realization of being my true self had emerged. The muscular structure of my chest area changed; the armoring had receded and the evidence was how far I could push my finger into my chest. My background in massage had proved useful for measuring my body for the changes from this work.

Those who will benefit from this transformational work are those who are hard on the spiritual path and want to advance faster, using an intense cleansing of the body armoring. Others will find a significant life changes, if they have had an abusive childhood or have experienced sexual abuse which affects their lives and emotions. Many can release, energetically, the abuse stored from decades past, also release the emotions and relearn and rewire them with much more insight. As children, we do not understand our parents reasons or motivation for what they have done to us. As adults, we can realign those distorted emotions in a new light and become ourselves again. We can have a new clear vision of how these emotions should have been all along.

This section is concerns interviews conducted with practitioners of Amanae who were trained in a nine month program.

Those interviewed are referred to by their initials, and mine are shown as KR the interviewer.

KR: What were your long term benefits for you from Amanae from the first class to further work??

PR   I have had a lot of work being in the nine month training program. It was clearing the body so that you can do the work and hold the space for people to do emotional releases, what ever their releases. I have some major things that sometimes seem subtle but are very big and basic. My trust in the universe is pretty complete, my self esteem has changed drastically. I can't imagine a situation where I would not feel good about myself, that is not to say I am competent about everything, but I feel OK about being incompetent. (laughter!)

KR.   You are accepting more about yourself, or your true self.

SR   I never really thought I had a self esteem problem before this. (Amanae) My connection with spirit is much stronger.   The most fun thing is that I can feel my heart open more and feel more of everything. (laugh) My health is much better. I had chronic fatigue at the start of the nine month program, just walking to my mail box was a lot. I was commuting

five hours to the program and after the first weekend my energy

changed drastically and was back up, although it was an up and down thing

but that is definitely gone.

KR   As a practitioner, what were your clients finding it beneficial for?

SR   There has not been all emotional release, there has been a lot of

spiritual integration. You have enough experience with the work to

know there is not always a sharing of what goes on, it is a personal

experience with yourself. I have people having spiritual experiences

such as having Jesus coming in and giving them messages and that

sort of thing. One woman accessed the Akashic records and they told her what

her life is about. Emotional release, sometimes of physical aliment

or muscular type occurs.

KR   When you went through your first classes, or the nine month training,

were you releasing childhood stuff or more with experiencing spiritual energies

or changes in that aspect?

SR   I had a fair amount of both. A lot of the emotional release was way

more than childhood stuff, but I got a real sense of the thread weaving of an

issue through lifetimes (past lives). For example there is a place in the upper

gullet, and someone touched it and I had an issue present time wise, then

back to my childhood and then suddenly it was an abandonment thing.

Suddenly I felt my jaw rotting and disintegrating and I was abandoned and left to die, then another event of abandon and left to die, and then I was left on a planet. It went back to layers and layers of separation. I am not one to dwell on past lives, I like to keep things present time.

KR   I met someone that every time they ran Reiki they got a vision of how they died in past life, I wouldn't want to do that!!

SR   One thing that I got, big time, from this is that -if we are going to change cellularly, and if we are going to be doing death differently perhaps by choice or not at all. If there are a lot of patterns in it cellularly and in mass consciousness that such and such happens..... then you start to age and die.   I was finding a real pattern relating to the chronic fatigue dealing with a certain issue and even a specific person interwoven with lots of lifetimes. Something would happen with them, and I would die.

KR   What about personal growth, was it more accelerated or more personal growth to you??

SR   That is all one. The more that you can accept and love and hold a place for yourself and your personality and issues , the more you can feel love in all areas. Through feeling and love is the connection to spirit and your divine self and clearing your body of a lot of patterns allows more light in. I also finished just a few weeks ago on "PAGE SEVEN" training.

KR   I recently had a private session with Christine with that. I was considering taking the training.

SR   It was awesome and I had an experience in there, but it was the most profound thing that ever happened in my life. We were doing this work and it was over, and Christine came over and laid her hand on me and said "Well, we are going to finish up now and go into meditation." I just sunk into this deep pit, and I felt effective. It felt like the core belief system, that was really the dysfunctional belief system of my life or lives. It was so hard to be there but I went to it and it was like an aspect of my self, and it was in there, and it was in there going, "You came here for me" (like visiting a dark aspect of the self). I just did not want to leave myself there, It was painful, very emotionally painful, but I went back there for three days.

Then one morning I had a dream about surrendering to love and I knew it was over, and I have been really different since.

KR   The system is very shamanistic and that describing of going into a pit or cave in the earth to finish work is not unusual. What would you say is the difference to you, how would you sum it up??

SR   I feel a much stronger closer connection with God and much more peace in my life. I could go on forever.

===
Second interview

KR   What do you think of the benefits from the first class or later?

ES   One of the biggest ones is reduction of fear. Fear is so

subtle, most people don't understand how much their lives are controlled

by fear.   Control is the right way to put it, not nicely but true. Fear

is not as prevalent, and I am not claiming to be without fear, some

fear is healthy. I am talking about the fear that you don't realize

you have! Something happens in your life and you suddenly feel

fear, and that is the amazing and powerful difference in the subtlety.

    Judgment, the lack of or less of that. For me when you

can judge everything and everyone in the same way, it is much easier

to be in the heart space.   The two go hand in hand, for me. I don't

have to try to judge and that does not mean that I am loving all the

time, but a greater acceptance of the way you are.   Those are the

two biggest ones. At a certain point, all my experiences that I have had

with energy and that through the Amanae, you go beyond those

experiences.   That does not mean that I am not open for those experiences,

but you don't lust for those, because if you are in the moment then the

moment unfolds.   That is another advantage that you can be in the moment,

which does relate in having a lessening of fear. Fear clamps down on energy.

KR   Blocking and armoring.

ES   Right , being in the flow a lot better. A lot of these are very powerful,

but the words to describe seem rather mundane. (KR.. inadequate)

Wow, I had this experiences, it was so fantastic, we came here and...

It is not that way! Although I have had some fantastic energy experiences and I appreciate them for what they are or what they were, but it's the long term that I am more into that opens up your awareness after a while. I think for me the benefits with Amanae continue on and that is why I stay with it. It could be argued that this is part of my contract or part of what I agreed to do when I came somewhat, that resonates pretty deeply within me and it is definitely a way to give back, even as a practitioner it has never been about making money, although I do charge for my services.

The real thing is to give back. I feel fortunate even before the Amanae I had a lot, to be thankful for. When I do a session on a person I really receive a lot and it is an honor to be permitted but not just the person I am giving the session to, but to be in their space. It is really not an awareness that you have right away, but as you continue with it you realize that, "I'm right in there" kind of thing. I am very privileged.

KR   As a practitioner, what kind or results or experiences do your clients have? There are different kinds of release and clearing.

ES   That depends. I've had people tell me things like they are more present and able to challenge authority figures. I have witnessed people in the two and five day, more in the five day classes, life changing things.   Have you done a five day thing and when?

KR   I did a five day first and then a two day. The five day about a year and a half ago.

ES   Then you know how powerful those can be.

KR   Oh YEAH!! (HA HA..)

ES   Do you think that you have ever gone back to the same?

KR   Gone back, no. Definitely it changed me. Changed my life certainly, releasing some of the armoring in my heart. It really had a lot to do with anger and fear of women. It was from the school teachers from the school system and I had no idea it was there. I had no idea the that bias or fear was subconsciously there all the time, causing me to have problems dealing with women in general. Oh yea it has made a change in life.

ES   A lot of it I don't remember, but the generalities are that they look and the energy change from day one to day five. I have talked to some of them six months later and, like you, they don't go back. They don't have to act differently but just be different.

KR   More of your true self.

ES   I don't think that it makes you a perfect person by any stretch of the imagination, what-ever the perfect person may be. It is not like you are without problems, and it is not like you are clear from five days, but they are powerful experiences for what you get in five days. It blows you mind. I am going up for a five day to construct and I learned to have no expectations or attachments, but I know it will be a powerful experience and people will get more than they can imagine. They may not get exactly what they wanted, and that is another thing about Amanae that is different. I used to think about spiritual growth, I used to have these pictures of the way I thought it would be, but my spiritual growth is not anything like I thought it might be. That does not mean that it is bad. It is amazing how the mind and ego can create pictures, of that and it just does not happen that way.

KR   Right, and there are so many paths, and it is hard to have any expectations on your path. (laughter)

ES   Other things people said to me were they could feel issues coming from the different doorways. They could feel things flow more, and they are more present in their body and just able to let go of things that held them back.

KR   What about spiritual aspects or changes, do your clients talk about that at all?

ES   Yes, one of my biases is that I had meditated for 25 years and I think that the Amanae had accomplished in maybe two years it equaled in what I had accomplished in the 25 years of spiritual growth. It is true that everyone on earth is on an accelerated path, but there are things that you can do that are not as accelerated as Amanae process. That may not make it suitable for everyone, I think it has something to offer for everybody, but not everybody is going to be willing to go through what Amanae is. Later, that may be different as time gets a little shorter, but yes, I think it is a very powerful and profound kind of thing. I have done a lot of extra work so my experiences may not be like everybody's. I did this first five day thing. I think it was the third or fourth day, I had this wonderful, what I called Pink energy come into my body. That was an incredibly beautiful experience. I have a lot of experiences of tremendous energies coming in.

KR   One of the things that I noted about this work and my own training is that I experienced energies and stuff coming from all the spiritual planes. The Buddhic, atmic, monadic and cosmic planes energies are present in the Amanae system.

ES   I definitely have a bias towards spiritual growth through the Amanae process, but then I came to realize that all growth is spiritual growth.

KR   Personal growth will lead you to spiritual growth.

ES   I have heard second stories of people that have seen Jesus and Sananda and others, all kind of different things open up to them in the process like the incredible love that comes through. If you arc open, but if you have tremendous expectations or attachments then you can block what comes through. I have had incredible experience of love when I put my hand on a person, I think it was a two day in Ukiah, maybe the one you were at. There were just incredible experiences that words can't cover. I agree, to me there has been a tremendous amount of spiritual expansion, that might be from the nine month practitioner training program.

KR   That is a pretty big commitment, and a whole other ball park of big advancement for you.

ES   The only way is to give sessions to people. It is not just learning how to do the movements, you have to have the clarity. If a person starts to shift, you might resonate if you still have a lot of your own stuff. You could not hold that space for them. Then I went ahead and did more work to open the heart even more, it's called the "Page Seven Process"

KR   I had a private session of that, so you liked that??

ES   Well... Oh Yeah. (laughter) That's one way to put it. Really it is another big commitment. I don't know how to put it, you go through another breakdown process of the ego letting go. I like the idea that the ego does not have to die, but it does have to take a back seat, that's good. I knew that 25 years ago when everybody wanted to kill the ego. Well, that does not feel right to me.

KR   Right, No one really wants a funeral.

ES   Taking a back seat is really an important thing....

KR   Surrender.

ES   It's exciting with the Page Seven, it has really added a new dimension to the Amanae work, or to the whole. It is one thing to come through the growth that you see that there are more steps that you have to take, there is no end. Everybody has to do as much as I can. That's another reason I am committed to the work. I'm doing it only because my private practice has not built up sufficiently on a part time basis, but in a minute I'd go full time. I think it is a question of getting the training and being ready for it when the time is right.

KR   That is very true. Just be patient with it, and it will come. Not many people have heard of Amanae, That is what is interesting to me. I have met a lot of people out there in the San Francisco Bay Area and virtually no one knows about the work. Only a handful have, because it is so new. It is just getting out there.

ES   Some of the people that experience it are frightened because it is so powerful. We just had a demo in Pleasanton, and I don't know if you have been to a demo recently, but Christine's energy is so pure. But when you have a room of over a hundred people and a lot of them are crying and shifting just from just what's happening on the table and no one is touching them, that can kind of put people off just a touch.

KR   I have done some free lectures on Subtle Energy and you have to accept that some people are not ready and some won't be ready for years.

ES   It's a seed, it is a seed planted. As time goes on, more people. As I understand the five day workshops are filling up a couple of months ahead. As more people are waking up more, I believe that is what it is. It is a destiny call, as Christine says. I think that is true because you have to be called somewhat. It is not an easy thing to say, " yeah ,

I don't know about this pain.... " but I am going to do it anyway.

There are people that come back for another five day workshop.

===

Third interview

KR   What got you started and what would you describe are the

first experiences with Amanae?

JB   It started about three years ago when a client of mine that

I had known for about 20 years came to me and said that they had

the most incredible bodywork the other day. As soon as she said

it, my body started vibrating. I said, "What is her name, where is

she and where do I get it?"

KR   You knew something was up.

JB   She said that she is very busy, she is booked months in advance,

she lives in Ukiah and comes down to Palo Alto once in a while. You have

to really book her far in advance. I called and booked an appointment,

three or four months in advance from the day I called.   Oddly enough

that appointment got messed up, and I never got that appointment,

Pat felt very badly and wanted me to meet Christine anyway and with my

schedule I could not wait and get a session later that day.

I met Christine and the first moment I met Christine I looked into her eyes and I thought, "Oh my God." She had the most amazing eyes.

That got all straightened out with the appointment and I got my first session

with her, and it was certainly phenomenal. I have had many kinds of peak

experiences with different kinds of venues, but nothing really touched

what happened on the table. I wanted more work, it was incredible.

She was booked months in advance, but Pat told me about the five

day workshop and I said, "sign me up."

That was the first time in my life that I had signed up for a workshop

without knowing anything about it, (Laughter) because the five day is so

different from a private session. They told me it would be intense, and

I had done EST and other things and I thought I knew what "intense," was

so I thought I could handle intense. That is lightly, it is more than intense

and the five day was so profound, the effects on me, that I wanted to do more

and I signed up for another session with Christine. During that period

they decided to start up the nine month practitioner program, and I knew

that I had to do that.

I was concerned about driving to Ukiah, but during a session with

Christine and while I was on the table I got a clear message from spirit that

this was my next step and just do it. I needed to not worry about the drive

and all those other things and I absolutely trust that this is meant to be.

I had never taken time off of work to take this sort of class, I trusted that

this would work and it worked out so amazingly. I could take off of work and pay my bills and do all the things that I needed to do and take the training.

KR   In your five day workshop what was the biggest impact, for me it was releasing childhood trauma's stuff, getting rid of that and bringing up issues I never knew stored in me.

JB   For me it wasn't so much the childhood issues because I don't think I was surprised by the issues that what came up during the five day workshop, but what I was surprised at was the incredible sense of love and oneness and the experience of that for the first time in my body ever. You know how every morning in class they ask you what your intentions are, getting those intentions every day for me.

KR   The messages were clear.

JB   Exactly, on the last day I wanted to experience divine love and I wanted to know it, really know it. (KR - That cosmic connection) Up until that point I had never volunteered for Christine's demonstration at the first part of class, I never once volunteered for that during the five days because I knew that Christine is ruthless. (laughter)

On the fifth day she asked for volunteers and my hand went up all by itself, it was like "Oh my God". She got me on the table and started with the heart as she does and in that moment on the table I got my intention.

AMANAE FOUNDATION www.amanae.com

Blank

CHAPTER SEVEN: EARTH ENERGIES

The earth is our lifeline, our home, our mother and our healing power tool
for clearing of negative energies that plague us. As a child I was amazed by water
springs that filtered the muddy rain to produce the clear wonderful tasting
liquid that flowed constantly from earth for drinking. Perhaps you have marveled
that the earth possesses this purification process built into the land, one that can clean
out the impurities in a short distance underground.

The earth has intelligence and is constantly showing us that it can take on negative
energies that we release. Ancient cultures had a much more intimate relationship
and knowledge of the earth's energetic aspects and its interaction with humans. The
concept of the planet having intelligence is common in the old days.

Geomancy is the study and use of etheric energies in the earth. These include "power
Points," ley lines and effects from underground water, streams and faults. The Asian arts call
it Feng Shui, which works with the balance of the yin and yang energies and their
affects on the surface of the earth. There is both western and eastern geomancy, each have
their own methods of application and goals. Dowsing is the most common application in the
west, although we have much to learn about this etheric access.

The etheric energies the earth breathes in and out are readily available to the power points. This constant breathing of the life and chemical ether of earth is part of what controls the weather. That is one big key that is missed by the weather service in discerning weather patterns. This has been explored by several scientists and has unheard of applications.

The earth produces incredible artistic communication outward with the crop circles and they show an intense geometric patterns similar to sacred geometry. These are incredibly complex, mathematically, and have profound visual effects. Many are too bizarre to "fake" quickly and correlate with the Magnetic fields changing in the 1990's. The earth resonance is going up (with some spikes) and the magnetic field is dropping!! Awakening to Zero point is a video to check out about some of the amazing changes taking place.

These Subtle Energies are mostly very thin and light in their effects, with a few exceptions. One of the most powerful and useful are the earth's power points. Only a small number of western people knew of these places of importance until recently. The earth flows the energy out of the point of the ley line intersections slightly, until special days of alignment called the "solstice." These are summer, winter, May Day and Halloween seasonal changes, like the longest summer day before the celestial change in the cycle. Scientists still have not grasped the meaning of the structures at the power points. Energy flows at power points like a tide change during the solstice, flowing out of the vortex power points.

Stonehenge and other "calendar" type monuments are a good example. Most archaeologists think the purpose is huge accurate calendar with the star alignment vectors at Stonehenge were for planting crops. WRONG! These structures were often built away from agricultural areas, and the farmers of that time would more likely look at the local plants to predict the time to plant the seeds, which is a much better indicator. The reason for a huge accurate calendar based on sun, star alignments was to place themselves at exactly the right time for the surge of etheric energy to flow through. This was a sacred time of ceremonial activity and is carried out all over Asia and other cultures by millions for spiritual and psychic activities. (See Geomancy books)

There is speculation that the pineal gland in the brain is a receiver of cosmic rays. The earth breathes in and out many spectrums of energy, causing stimulating effects to our hidden receptors. Subtle energy systems often pull energies from the cosmos such as specific stars and even the solar logos. It makes sense that with the earth's cycles of seasons, the shift of energies would occur at the solstice, or change of season. Astral alignments also affect this pull on the earth's storage and flowing like spinning a wet sponge in a circle)

These powerful sources of energy may be a result of the many things flow into the earth such as gravity, solar emissions, and magnetic field energies. Various "Earth" energies emerge at different points and give different reactions to the individual at these locations. It can release emotions, heal and give "visions" to the person tuned to this power. I doubt that it will fix your VW beetle's water pump problem, so don't get too excited! The characteristics vary with each power point and Martin Gray has given one of the best descriptions of what each point can do for you. You may have extraordinary experiences, AS I HAD!

The popular power point today is in Sedona which is a hot tourist spot, although there are many all over the planet. A power point may have several outlets in one area, such as springs, rock outcroppings and often mountain tops. This is why stories of "gurus" that go to the mountain top, meditate and draw energy. The Bible refers often to important miracles on mountain tops. The Sermon on the Mount, Mount Lebanon, Jesus ascended from the top of a mountain and Moses went up on the mount.

In American history such sites are the sacred land of native American Indians, please respect them and honor the ceremonies held there for the spiritual aspects of these earth people. These power points are very valuable to us if we can educate ourselves on the proper uses of energy for good of all and not for selfish reasons like greed or lower frequency things.

One theory of the Russians is that there is a giant crystal structure in the earth's core (maybe the hot iron core solidified OR spinning inside a Geo- structure) Power points are at the peak of the points of this multifaceted shape. This makes sense when you look at the large number of them along the north and south, 30'th parallel of the earth's latitudes. This includes the pyramids, also Native American Indian sacred places,   I predict there wil be a rash of them discovered in the South American jungles in the near future, along the southern 30'th parallel or those ley lines.

We are tuned into the earth through the iron in our blood. This connection was noticed by Wilhelm Reich and Orgone accumulators in their structure of steel, or steel wool for collecting life energy. Reich avoided using other metals because of our compatibility with the iron metal which is the supposed core of the earth.   Crystal structures are known to resonate in similar ways, sympathetically, and we resonate with the earth when doing healing work. It is often seen that our brain waves link up the earth's resonance, or Shuman rate of 7.8 to 8 cycles per second when doing healing energy flows. Today we see a shifting in this frequency as well as magnetic fields. (See Awakening to Zero Point.)

Our ancient ancestors were more in tune the Earth with their connections. They used The Pyramids all over the earth to ground the energies to the earth's dimensions. They also used Obelisks in many forms all over the planet, and someone did on Mars too. They knew things that make you wonder and envy their wisdom. This knowledge is part of us, in the very DNA from our ancestors.

Think about the science involved in the design and building of the pyramids! This was not "primitive culture baby steps". There were some serious, math-loving people involved in the structure with all of it's proportions. The shape of the great pyramids show a sophisticated device combining many features in one structure. It is a tuning device proportioned to the earth's dimensions used itself to tune the earth and it's celestial resonances. Pyramids may be located over specific power points that, in their time have been useful for several applications.

Cultures more in tune with nature and its subtle energies know how to find power points through the feeling in their bodies and perhaps a dowsing instrument. In Europe, they marked the power points with a stone that often stood up. This made it easier to find it later, while doing nomadic traveling. These swirling vortexes of power were used before the Roman Christians occupied Europe. When the church tried to convert the people, they kept returning to their favorite sacred place, against the priest's strict orders. The first attempts to eradicate this "superstition" were to break up the rocks marking the point. Then, Roman orders came down to keep the locals happy while "lording over them" through conversion to Christianity.

The church leaders soon got the clue to build a new church on the power point and sensed the energies with ley lines radiating from them. When the order came from the Vatican, churches were built over the original rock marking the spot. The locals could come to the spot, be healed, feel good, and the church could call it "Mary's healing rock "or some such. The structure was lined up so that the center aisle followed ley lines out the door and down the street up to the front of the church. Previously called the devils work, now is "the church's healing" when parishioners pray to the saint there. These miracle cures were pointed out to be from saint "so-and-so," Mother Mary or Jesus.
(Geomancy books are highly recommended!)

I had no concept of this when I went to churches on vacation in Europe. I went to the Notre Dame church in Paris and stepped inside. An emotional feeling of pleasant admiration and awe came over me. The statues were beautiful and the emotional release continued and became more intense until I left. A similar thing happened in the art museum called the Petite Palace also in Paris. Different emotions were drawn out at each place I visited. It was not until years later that I learned these places were built on power points which was the cause of my reaction, not the art I had observed. At an art museum in Italy where eight to ten percent of those visiting leave the place crying or catatonic. This is due to the various characteristics of the power point energies and frequencies.

The Christians played this "to the Max" by having pilgrimages to and from the churches across Europe to see "relics of saints" and be blessed.   In other countries it is still common for large masses of religious pilgrimages to take place at holy places. It died out in Europe hundreds of years ago with a few exceptions.

Many springs and spas carry the life energy and are know to have healing properties. This is common in all parts of the world where people flock and pay a fee to soak in the right spot or spa for your ailments.   There is more than the mineral content in these waters or mud baths. Some of the spa's earth energy has healing properties for some conditions better than others, say for arthritis or organ problems. The important point is the energies emitted at these power points are not all the same, but carry frequencies tuned to that part of the body in need. A location that heals one person may not contribute to another's healing.   This vibrational resonance is covered in great detail in the book "Vibrational Medicine." This may also have parallels in the radionics field.

Most may not feel anything at these "power places," but the more time spent, the more you will develop a sensitivity to these energies. The ancient cultures chose one extra-sensitive person, who had dealt with the subtle energies, and chosen for their ability to experience it. These were the shamans and wizards who could best use the power for healing or seeing into the unknown.

Martin Grey's book and his lectures on "Planetary Acupuncture" is the best explanation of this, as he traveled 70 countries and visited 700 power points. He describes many different uses and huge populations who use the one day a year to perform religious ceremonies at such places experiencing unbelievable things. There are many religions, cultures and races that use these power points for the benefit of the people.

Today, the practice of geomancy and Chinese Feng Shui are used in deciding where building should be on the property. Dowsing for problem energies like two streams crossing under a house, and moving furniture to distance yourself from bad energies is being done much more by professional geomancers here in America. If your scientific mind says "piffel poof" to these dowsing methods, consider that they have been used for centuries in China and is used every day here in the United States for many purposes. Real estate companies are using Feng Shui for preparing properties before selling, or improving them for a sale.

Hold back your judgment on things you have no experience or knowledge of. There are scientific reports on all of these dowsing devices and their accuracy when used in the right hands. There is an American Association of Dowsers and many books on the subject, and there are many active persons and advanced methods to use.

There are positive and negative power points on the earth also. A rare one in Santa Cruz County, California is called the "Mystery Spot". This is a place were gravity is warped and the compass sits off of north by 90 degrees in places. As I entered the area's boundary, I had a feeling of anxiety like a blanket of depression come over me. I then read the sign of how it was discovered by the early owners. When they stepped onto that part of the property they felt the emotional change and tried to figure it out. Once I was told the exact border line to cross, I moved out, and the feeling disappeared. I have talked to others who are sensitive to the energy, the odd feeling stayed with them for hours or days afterwards, and usually, they did not want to return. I have done some interesting and bizarre experiments at the Mystery Spot and have used a magnetic vitic generator to cancel out the effect, and used it to reverse the negative effects of the area.

A phenomena I've heard of is that the points are positive and negative at different times of the year. The sun spots have been correlated to the alignment of the planets (RCA Radio knows this, but not many others) The sun spots are responsible for magnetic storms, and magnetic storms may cause outbreaks of anger, violence and wars, according to correlation studies in Burl Payne's book - The Body Magnetic. Perhaps this is from too much hot yang energy released by the sun causing warfare among the planet's population. The solar system and planets have influence on the earth and may shift the energy streams out of the power points.

What do inquiring minds do with this? Stay away from magazines in the checkout Lines, that's for sure! Try the dowsing books and clubs to learn the delicate art of geomancy. The scientific evidence is hot and heavy on both sides when it comes to proof of the ability of dowsing. Try it, and you may find yourself to be a very good operator. The person operating the instrument is often the key to the success of dowsing, so to find out if you are more receptive, try it. Give yourself time, and practice daily for weeks or months to develop the skill, the same as with a musical instrument.

When you have a chance, stop by the positive power points and see if they affect you, then if you can travel there at the summer solstice go for it. Do your own experiments if you feel the emotions, and open your mind to a new world. Try it when your Bio rhythms are at their triple peak, too! We can release much negative energy to the earth for healing and it is very powerful for purification.

Using the earth's energy is a matter of grounding and pulling up energy in your healing work. This is enhanced at power points, as well as making it easier to send negative

101

energies into the ground. There is an attunement in the Huna healing system to enable you to ground better and link to the core of the earth and its energies. Huna is a very heart oriented and grounded system that believes we need to be comfortable in our bodies.

The best use of power points is for the location for practicing meditations. You can connect more with the earth when dwelling at the power points. People traveled to these sacred places during solstices to gain visions of the future and communicate with celestial beings. If you have health problems, go to the power points and run subtle energies such as Reiki or Spiritual Unfoldment Network systems, especially in hot pools known to have healing properties.

Some locations have retreats and lodging where you can stay for a while, also classes and workshops on stress reduction and massage. If you have time and need more work, you may want to consider taking up residence and working part time at such retreats. This gives you the advantage of living at the power point with constant access to the healing energies.

There are many classes on geomancy and Feng Shui, go out there and look around A professional geomancer can come out to your house or place of business and test for underground streams that may affect your immune system by pulling it down with too much yin or yang energy. Welcome these new arts with their unexplored possibilities, they are very useful for spiritual advancement. Seek the power points and try doing activities there for a few days or a week. Then ask yourself about the changes within you. Some power points I have visited gave me endless energy, I need less sleep, this is the effect on my body. See what it can do for you. You may have visions of the future as did the ancient Shamans did.

Reference -   The Art of Geomancy

Reference -   Geosphere magazine. Version #5, September, 1983

Reference -   Pulse of the Planet - Trevor Constable

Reference -   Vibrational Medicine - Richard Gerber, MD
                          Bear and Company   Santa Fe NM. 87504-2860
Reference -   Planetary Acupuncture - Martin Gray

Reference -   Burl Payne Body Magnetic -
                          Body Mind connection   1108 Spruce St.
                          Boulder, CO. 80302

Sedona has many power points that
are very powerful and vary in character.
Visitor information   Sedona AZ.
8 Sedona Oak Cr. Canyon
Chamber of commerce
P O Box 478
Sedona AZ.

Healing Energy Power Points in California:

Harbin Hot springs

Esalon

Wilbur Hot springs

Sierra Hot springs

Orr Hot springs.
BOOK: HOT SPRINGS OF THE WEST.

Blank

CHAPTER EIGHT: WHAT DOES SCIENCE SAY ABOUT IT ALL?

Modern science says much about subtle energy, ether energy, life energy, but few believe or listen to what these great scientists have to say. Tremendous discoveries have been suppressed, ignored or blatantly destroyed in order to protect invested business interests and / or medical technology. Science is now taking a second look and is slowly changing its mind, but this is like turning an ocean liner around to a new direction. It will take time.

Western science does not like "Ether Energy" or subtle energy because some say that it comes from "another dimension". This "magical place" is not acceptable to analytical science due to lack of proof. However, the growing handfuls of "Quantum scientists" now are seeing a much different world from what we learned in college and high school. Theories of parallel universes have been proved quite possible and are gaining.

If you study the scientists from about 200 years ago, you will find that most of them believed in some sort of ether energy. Some of the modern scientists have pushed its existence with little success, Nicoli Tesla is one. Scientists like Plato, Newton, Faraday, many others, were believers in the ether energies and what they could do. Why do modern scientists differ? Some of this is education, if you are taught a "law" of physics, you will probably never try to break it. Other countries have a different attitude thus they have made great inroads. Some have scientific systems that date back 3,000 years or more, they also have much evidence that subtle energy can be manipulated to benefit health.

In Asian systems there are five elements: Earth, Water, Fire, Air and "Ether." To describe the element Ether you would have to name as many characteristics, for example the element water. Water can be clean and rain from the sky, or it can be murky like the Mississippi River. You may have clear water to wash your face, or get splashed by a mud puddle in New York City. To define the element ether is to look at the many characteristics and traits as found in any of the other four elements.

The scientific community now looks at the vacuum energy, another name for ether energy. The Ether name is one to be avoided in the physics industry, unless you wish to loose your job or grant money. Now it is called the vacuum energy, therefore they do not have to admit they made a mistake years ago when they wrote ether off as "nonexistent."

The scientific community found "free" energy floating around in a vacuum, which they called vacuum energy. The concept is simple: in outer space there must be a medium for light to pass from the stars, because of the wave theory of light. To have waves, there must be a medium. If you throw a rock into a pond, it makes waves. If there is no water in the pond, mud does not make waves. Simply put: SPACE IS NOT EMPTY!

Remember, you're not in Kansas anymore and the scientist's names and terms will not be familiar, but stick with the Yellow Brick Road for the tornado is just starting. Hang loose with Toto, for your adventure is upon you.

Scientist name	Term for energy:
L.E. Eeman	X force
Wilhelm Reich	Orgone or life energy
C. Von Rickenbach	Odic force
Francis Mesmer	Animal Magnetism
Rudolph Steiner	Life Force or Ether body
John Keely	Spirit
Russian Science	Bio-energy
Asian Science	CHI
India	Prana

To arrive at a definition of the Subtle energies you must think of a substance so small it is less than the size of the electron. It is more like light that sits still or moves slowly, and can be seen only by special methods. If you build a pile of it by concentrating it, then it can be fully visible to the human eye under darker conditions. Many scientists and ancient cultures worked and played with these energies and produced vast evidence of its existence and the sources of its origin. Compared to the neutrino, it is also small enough to be very elusive and hard to detect.

Some Etheric Sources :

-SUN: the sun emits tremendous power in many spectrums. If you think of energy coming from the sun in the form of heat, light and the photosynthesis for all the plants on earth, all together it is only one billionth of what is sent out by the sun into solar system. OH, and we have a smaller star! The sun puts out neutrinos, light, gamma, ultraviolet, infrared, x-rays and many others. It puts out tremendous etheric energy in large amounts, solar prana.

-EARTH: The earth takes in many things, including gravity, neutrinos and magnetic fields. What does it put out? From power points on the surface, it pushes up energy vortexes, more at certain times of the year, mainly at the solstices. Geomancy is the study of earth energies through many methods. You can develop a sensitivity to the earth energies and use it for dowsing a particular underground item. Most cultures have used dowsing for centuries, in China they often consult the Feng Shui practitioner before constructing a new building to see if it matches well with the nature of the land. Building designs are even changed to accommodate the nature of the land.

-GENERATORS: Devices available from sources like "Borderland Science" and "Tools for Exploration" put out the energy at certain rates. These little generators have no moving parts and some use magnets to pull etheric energy from the magnetic interactions and the human body. They can be used for enhancing your own energy, and will pick you up when your energy is down.Some of this is the result of discoveries from the Egyptians who knew many things of an advanced scientific nature. Egyptian mummies were found to have a crook and flail in their hands which were a disguise for a rod of carbon and a rod of magnetic lodestone. Held in the hands, these give an energetic feeling and it makes a great replacement for coffee to wake up!

-CONCENTRATORS and FOCUSING: pyramids, spiral coils, and crystal tools. (lasers are crystal based). The pyramid of Cheops may have been used as a ram water pump, and also to energize the water for the improvement of agricultural crop growth.

The Borderland Science Magazine has articles about this.

-PEOPLE: People have had the ability to heal with the "laying on of hands." Most religions have miracles that changed the molecular structures in a flash. Today there is a return to therapeutic touch in nursing, Reiki from Japan. Acupuncture pushes the energy around the body to tune it up, like tweaking an analog electronics system. Groups can build the life energy charge in large amounts with the use of spiritual dances and rituals with exotic purposes. You too can tap into the "wall of light" that many scientists know about.

What can it be used for today? An east European man found that a razor could be sharpened by placing it beneath a pyramid shape aligned north, and he was granted a patent for sharpening blades. Next, the pyramid could be used for just about anything, such as making your Volvo engine block last longer. Many wild claims became known but one was quite valuable to the ancient cultures. This was proved by several experiments with seeds "charged" under the pyramid shape, which make them sprout and grow faster and larger. One theory now gaining momentum is that the great pyramid was once a huge ram water pump that treated the water that was used to humidify the desert air and water the fertile desert crops.(Czechoslovakian patent #91304.)

Charged crop seeds and water would be a big advantage to a city population with people who need a good agricultural base. Two scientists at different locations arrived at the theory of the huge pyramid ram water pump. Further investigations may tie other theories on free energy power involved in flowing water through the system. These are shown in Borderland Magazine, Box 220, Bayside California. 95524.

In order to have a large city population, in that particular country, they must have powerful agricultural farming to feed the masses. The health of the people and all society is often tied to the strength of the food chain. To be able to grow better crops with "charged water" is of great value to the early Egyptian population's well being, more so in the desert.

Ancient healers through-out time used a technique of pushing a special energy out of the hands which gives life energy to the sick, and causes amazing results. A wonderful saying by Edgar Cayce is "Vibration is that same energy, same power, ye call God". Much of these techniques lay dormant in the esoteric writings of eastern and western countries. The mystical paths to gain access and attune to these energy frequencies are being opened up and are accessible to all who want it.

There are numerous scientific studies about the effects of subtle energies, but mainstream medicine and science in down plays them or ignores them. Laying on of hands increases good enzymes while reducing bad enzymes. Studies at Stanford University show these energies can penetrate a foot of lead. Other scientific studies show effects of distant healing from thousands of miles away on cloud chambers in a lab. Acupuncturists have measurement devices for the Chi that they manipulate and this is slowly being accepted by the medical field. The evidence is there, but it will take time for people to adapt their thinking.

Scientists like Lahovski cured chronic diseases with an electrical Multiple Wave Oscillator. Wilhelm Reich could reduce cancer growth and reverse early cancers with a simple accumulator device. Ruth Drown could diagnose diseases and cure them with a box of variable resistors without electricity! Most of this was done through sympathetic vibrations of just the right frequency. Some scientists could control the weather with mechanical devices that draw off the atmospheric ether energy from the sky and clouds. They could also bring green plants to the desert.

Wilhelm Reich gives a good explanation of why the mainstream science and society rejects and condemns the evidence of life energy (and subtle energy). Refer to Reich's book "The Emotional Plague." Much of this involves deep psychology and the armoring that many people in our society carry with them, restricts the energy within them. Those with authoritarian backgrounds tend to suppress the life energy and smother those promoting access to it.

Some scientists gave more than their time and money to develop and discover applications. They gave their flesh and blood. Some were persecuted to death, it is our honor to seek out the truth, so that we all can benefit and advance our human evolution. Seek the truth beyond what the schools and business want for their financial gain, and you will have pride in your work. You can make a name for yourself by pushing the boarders of both science and spirit.

Exotic devices described and demonstrated by Tesla and John Keely have shown that actual electrical power can be pulled from ether, or the wall of light as it is described. Today, science investigates the "vacuum energy" that Tesla and Keely played with over 100 years ago! For years the earth energy was tapped into, using underground plates to charge the old fashioned batteries used by the phone company . Earth batteries were used by the telephone industry to power long distance communication lines. This was free energy from the earth in low voltages - that were used to power circuits.

Free energy devices have been shown and some have demonstrated the ability well, few revealed the clues that are keys to a revolution in free power. The creators taking the secrets to the grave. They may not be simply tapping into the "wall of light" but also through vibrational releasing of the etheric energy into physical mechanical energy.

Tesla transmitted power without lines and had only a three percent loss through the air, but he advocated providing free electrical power to people all around the world. This caused backers like Edison, Westinghouse and others to pull back their funding and support because this meant no money in it for them, once the systems were built. It's always sad when money gets in the way of a great idea and screws it up. Who wants to give electrical power away when you can sell it to generations of people! (In California) Free power may not be a blessing, because power corrupts, thus free power may create a more wasteful society that is not ready for it. Often, technical advancements are grabbed up by the military for destructive purposes used by governments. We already have enough abilities and talents in this area. Go boldly forth, study, and the truth will come out as to how little we know about our universe, and how much value there is in the ancient knowledge.

Religion has used earth energy power points for ritual ceremonies to increase higher consciousness and see visions of worlds unknown. Yes, even the Catholic church uses etheric energies that they will tell you is "the devils work," if not applied by them. If you believe this is rarely used by religions, then read about the pilgrimages in Asia. In India, one location every four years is used as a stopping point for 11 (or more) MILLION people for several days to worship at the energy point. They know this is a very important place, and the correct time to perform many religious actions and make big spiritual advancements.

Church steeples and spires are an antennae to focus life energy collected within the congregation. This is of benefit to those who are not sensitive to the energies.

One parallel is that between what eastern masters teach about the energy centers in the body called "Chakras" and the view of Wilhelm Reich. Reich found that centers of the flow of life energy along the spine became constricted by tension and also was a source of neurosis. This led to Armoring, which held back the flow of our all important life energy, needed both for good health and good sexual response. The person who restricts themselves or is too restrictive in their daily life, (authoritarian upbringing) would, therefore, contract repeatedly and also restrict the energy flow and have poor sexual energies. Opening these closed chakra valves is a key to good health and a good sex life, as well as an important part of cancer prevention.

In Chinese and Tibetan cultures life energy is called Chi, Ki, and Prana. In Acupuncture the lack of flow in the body is called stagnation is associated with disease or weakened body functions. When the American Medical Association lost the battle to keep acupuncture from Asia, many of the theories of the old order died. Proof of no life energy, or chi in the body, went out the window. Now we have much more clinical evidence that these oriental healing arts are indeed powerful for many ailments.

Western medical science did not believe that there were meridians used in acupuncture until someone took a closer look with an electron microscope and found them. There is also a system of Nadis (plumbing) that is also something new to western medicine. The medical industry had separated the mind and body when treating them; now they realize they are all connected in one big blob. They do not want to admit to any connection between

113

subtle energies affecting both mind and body rhythms. Change is coming: one group pushing subtle energies in the medical profession is ISSSEEM (International Society for the Study of Subtle Energies and Energy Medicine). Phone 303-278-2228

The days of suppression of evidence supporting the life energy are fading fast Usually students emerging from college today do not have the knowledge contained in this book. In order to catch up, you will have to dig deep into the ancient books from great scientists of the past, and learn from them. You attend school to keep from reinventing the wheel, learn from other's mistakes, and how to avoid them. This is now catch-up time for today's scientists. Fortunately in America we have a vast cultural diversity to learn from.

Scientists sins of the past can be forgiven. Western science ignored evidence of life energy and made the mistake of not looking further and deeper at physical results from using life energy. Around the turn of the century there was a series of experiments done that had "disproved" existence of ether. The series is referred to as the "Martin Morley" experiment. Several other western scientists became involved like Einstein.

It was really an experiment that looked for life energy visually with a "interferometer" device that is used for adding and subtracting of waves. It also looked not to prove the existence of ether, but to determine if the earth's rotation pulled the ether along with it on the surface, somewhat like a blanket over the face of the earth.

I am afraid that this was like looking for a magnetic field with a pair of binoculars. Somehow you will probably overlook the photons moving and observe more interesting things in the apartment complex next to the science lab. Russians have photographed the results of the ether energy affecting electrons in the form of the Kirlian photographs of the aura in living things. This is more concrete than most, but still not acceptable in mainstream science. Seeing the ether energy is very hard, much like an example of finding the particles out there that we theorize. Gathering evidence for a small item is not easy. For example the years and big money it took to prove that the theoretical neutrino was real.

To locate a neutrino was an interesting experiment. Looking for them must be one of the toughest jobs in the world, and I have tremendous respect for those who set out to prove that the neutrino exists. Proof was found with several tests done, which took many years to produce required evidence. The argument is: how many of them are there, and how often do they pulse out of the sun? This is an example of how difficult it is to look at minute sub atomic particles. Search for the brother or sister of a neutrino and you are looking for something very hard to establish, that is if your instruments are not built or modified to look for the subtle energy.

The western world of science has been infatuated with finding basic building blocks or elements of matter since before the time of Newton. Modern physics scientists look at the makeup of molecules with the particle collider. They are simply a big electron gun (like your TV set) that smashes the particles together, the end product is a "heavy little bugger" that lasts only nanoseconds. This is long enough to see that they are different from all other existing molecules and compounds on earth, but that they are heavier than the electron, proton, and neutron. This does not explain about which things must combine to form the electron. Theories are startling and will blow away laws that we learned in college physics classes when the truth comes is revealed! See Fred Wolf's book on parallel universes to shake your physics foundation.

One big reason that there has been little attention by the science community toward life energy is most in the scientific community have been hired by business to build death devices for financial gain. With the defense-offense industry as one of the worlds largest employers, the emphasis in our schools and universities has been to manufacture good destructors. With the "peace dividend" around the corner, if politicians will keep out of it, we can use our science talents to push out more life energy, healing products and of course, students. We must find incentives to get big business to invest and explore unknown areas universities must also shift their thinking around to new goals. Keep this in mind as a consumer!

A big difference in the medical directions of east and west is that the western world wants to kill everything! Antibiotics, surgery, radiation to destroy the invader, sounds like a start for a Monty Python movie. In the east, the emphasis is on strengthening the body and immune system to fight off the invading monster the way nature intended. A problem with western antibiotic medicine is that it does not keep ahead of the adaptability of germs and is becoming a King Kong monster. We are talking RADICAL CHANGES in attitude here. There is surgery and western medicine in China, but with acupuncture there is a better balance of coverage of problems.

Heads of authority will not change easily. Think how much work is involved with changing the text books when a law is proven wrong. If a genius emerges who breaks the second law of thermodynamics and creates heat from "nothing" imagine how many scientist it will take to edit all those college text books and explain how the law changed. Who would want that job? They will whine and suppress evidence and resist the change and not adapt unless it is demanded of they by authority. Truth is hard to accept when previous laws have been broken. A broken law of physics is like a fairy tale that turned out to be wrong.

A bizarre book came out in the 40's about how a hundred scientists argued against Einstein's theories. Reflecting back, it should be called "100 Bozos on this Bus to the Boston Brick yard" by Nonu Nutons. It is easy to laugh with hindsight at such goofy book, but at that time these scientists were quite serious and cemented in their "Newtonian physics overshoes." Lesson one: BE ADAPTIVE!

Fear of the unknown, and results of those changes are the other side of the spectrum. When we change or advance, part of us must "die"! This is the basis of many rituals throughout the world. When people go through ceremonies like confirmation, marriage, graduation, and other maturing rituals, the former person "dies" and is substituted by a new one. This is evident in cultures where one may actually change their name after the ritual. Which for signifies that you are forever modified and you are reminded of that change each time you hear or repeat your name. I now accept name changing in the 60's and 70's by friends which signify the depth of change in their life's direction. Joseph Campbell's work tells us that we need more of these rituals and that the lack of these maturity steps is the source of many social problems. So change with life, and be willing to bend with the wind in all the directions!

Science must adapt and move forward in life energy work. If you open up positive paths for mankind, then this requires changes in all attitudes and walks of life. Sidestep the swamps and quicksand, be willing to change, and you will find a treasure with which to improve your life, though you will have to jump high when life says "jump!"

Three clear hurdles must be overcome by the radical scientist in order to make changes for the better of humankind:

1. When the scientist discovers new things, they must create a new set of words and terms, sometimes even a new language with translation. This was John Keely's problem. He was so far ahead of other scientists in 1900 that they had a hard time understanding what he was talking about! Communication is difficult, it seems simple until you get a suburbanite from London with a cockney accent trying to speak to a Singapore factory worker on pigeon English. They both use the English language, but they may be able to understand only 10 % of the important stuff.

Creating a new language or set of terms is not easy, consider English, it is always a good source of jokes for professional comedians. Everyone who uses them must understand your new terms, especially the investors who will bring the fruit to market.

2. The scientist must then convince a large group of other scientists to become accepted by the "main stream" and thus gain financial support for further study and application. There are stories of vast discoveries that languished on the sidelines until the need grew so large it create a vacuum. (Like Ross Perot's great sucking sound!) This is pointed out well in the Megabrain journal article showing that the hot scientist needs to convince other scientists by their studies. These studies must consist of a large number of subjects and the cost (even at a university) can run into tens of thousands of dollars. A new inventor or company can't afford such costs to prove their devices. This becomes harder and more expensive if you want to be approved by medical organizations who require extensive

double blind studies at their favorite facility.

3.   The final high hurtle will be to convince a financially stable investor to invest in the

mass production of products that will improve all our lives. If the business community can't

understand the scientist's language, it will never learn the value of that discovery.

This also keys in on fear, if a business person fears change or loss of their old business or

business image, to a new and exotic product, they will not invest their capitol in the

production or development. This is called the "get a horse" syndrome.

The investment and science community are more closely linked in today's

information age of the computer and telecommunications. This will continue to break down

barriers of the past with more sharing of realities and data spurring greater communication.

We must all change and flow easier with all of the shifting tides. Help to open doors

and push back the barriers that restrain us in life energy work! To adapt is not easy, but it is

always worth it. Many things in life scare us at first until we understand it.

When confronted with the first steam shovel, some laborers cried it would put 100

men wielding shovels out of work. Franklin Roosevelt's reply was, Yes, or a thousand men

with teaspoons out of work. Progress usually means a threat to someone, even if it takes

the burden off of their broken back. The computer is a good example of fear of the

unknown.

Einstein had a schoolmaster who told him that he'd "never amount to anything." He

did not listen to that school master. Don't let the mistaken opinions of others deter you.

Opinions can be rejected. Try it... Einstein did not talk until he was three, therefore

his parents thought he was retarded and took him to a doctor. Even his parents did not believe in him. Science is changing and in time evidence will support the theory and belief in the subtle energies. There are groups who are fighting this uphill battle with a blazing banner against an established educational system and stodgy scientists.

Many ask if there is scientific evidence exists to support subtle energies and there is plenty but the reality is that some people put too much emphasis on the scientific community being able to save us from all our problems. We must look at ourselves and inside ourselves to find sources of these problems. We also must take for granted that these energies do exist and proceed with the practical part of life by putting it them work for us. We should saturate ourselves, bathe in it's finer essence, and learn to love more. Science should also look at the spiritual as an integral aspect of the complete picture, Einstein did

Books:
Tao of Physics by Fritjof Capra

Parallel Universes by Fred Allen Wolf.

Borderland Science article 1993 spring,
        Pyramid pump
         Borderland Science
Vibrational Medicine by
        Richard Gerber   Bear and co.

Book/lecture: Planetary Acupuncture, Martin Gray
ISSSEEM
        International Society for the Study of Subtle
        Energies and Energy Medicine.
        356 Goldco Circle
        Golden, CO 80403   303-278-2228.
        Science and medicine organization for advancement
        in uses of energies integrated into treatments.

CHAPTER NINE: TANTRA AND TAOIST COSMIC CONNECTION.

Love is all you need. Perhaps the greatest subtle energies are those that circulate within the body. The advantages of cultivating and circulating them are tremendous. Ancient secrets used by the great mystery schools are now becoming available to the public, which we can take advantage of them in our daily lives. You may harness the powerhouse in your body to create much more pleasure in your sex life, and to improve your spirituality. Few know how to change sexual energy into spiritual energy, but you will by the end of this chapter. Best of all, the cost is only how much of your time you wish to invest. You won't have to purchase new bedroom toys or approach your mail box furtively.

If I said you could improve your sex life by having multiple orgasms, more sensitivity and longer periods of lovemaking you might be interested. You may find this new path you are embarking on will give you far more intense romance with all your partners in the future, and also bring improved health. This is often how Tantra is sold in the western world. It carries the connotation of intensifying sexual pleasure. Most who first encounter this see it as "SEX" only as they have never thought of sex as a powerful path to spirituality.

On the other hand, if I told you that without any help from a priest or guru you can push your spiritual advancement and connect deeply with your higher self, you might be interested. That path appeals to you if you have been turned off by churches and dogma associated with Victorian attitudes about sex being just for procreation. Tantra in the eastern countries is not about sex as much as a spiritually minded practice to enhance our reaching out to the cosmic plane with it's wonderful benefits. To the eastern practitioner it is a spiritual tradition that works and has advantages over other methods that take longer.

The techniques for cultivating the sexual energy, for most, have never been revealed to us or our parents, therefore we have no concept of what it can do for us. If someone told me five years ago that I could have several orgasms an hour as a man, I would have thought they were into selling snake oil or Florida swamp land. Today, I will never return to "conventional" sex methods for they are now unsatisfactory. These techniques are not "kinky" or require exotic equipment but are exercises that anyone can do. If I have convinced you to try and invest the time to get there, just go to the references and pick out a book that can give you all the details.

As a woman you may be interested in the lessening effects of PMS and the improved health aspects. You can control the quality of life during both the Monthly "Curse" and strengthen muscles for child birth and love making. Look at the book "Healing Love Through the Tao: Cultivating Female Sexual Energy. Mantak and Maneewan Chia. Healing Tao books.

The most basic method brings up spiritual energies and sends some of it to your higher self and feeds them power for their benefit. When you consistently send energies to the higher self there are many advantages, better health, longevity and you become more connected with your solar Angel. In the Hawaiian Huna system the lower self sends Mana (CHI) to the higher self to accomplish a deed or request and in many magical systems the energy in the spine is vectored up to manifest things. The term Christ came from the Roman term "Christe," having to do with bringing up energy through the spine. These all use the Nadi strands similar to the meridians in the body, but transfer and channel energies.

One simple but very effective technique is covered in the Mantac Chia book series on cultivating sexual energy in the micro cosmic orbit. This should be done daily for at least 10 minutes and followed for several months, so one should make the time and discipline for this work. It will not only enhance sex, but will strengthen spirituality. This exercise is to increase longevity, health and strength. (Mantak Chia books on male energy)

For a brief description of the microcosmic orbit, you can draw up the spine (through the NADI's) sexual energy from the sex organs and loop it around the top of the head. It is then directed downward through the top of the mouth, (gate) with the tongue to the top of the mouth, it flows

down the front of the body to the spleen chakra (below the naval or second chakra).

Along with contracting the perineum on the in breath and drawing

energy up the spine, you then relax and breath out while energy flows down the front.

In this journey through the microcosmic orbit sexual energy is changed into

life energy, then into spiritual energy to build a greater spirit body.

The complete technique is described in several books by Mantac

Chia and Mewan Chia and through their classes on these methods.

Using various techniques in these books, you can increase your internal

CHI power which will magnetically attract others who have similar energies to share

and have balanced friendships. When you attract those who also use the same techniques

you may discover a powerful spiritual bond with lasting power. Strengthening

the spirit body with energy can help when accessing energies and other

dimensions for channeling. According to science we are resonators in many

respects. Our bones are crystalline and resonate with a piezo-electric affect.

Use your body in an new way and find the increased longevity,

used secretly for centuries used by the Asian elite. I've also heard that

some of these techniques can be found in the Bible and in other religious

documents used around the world.

Western Tantric practices are usually taught to those who wish

to improve their sexual relations and enhance relationships. Spiritual

aspects are becoming revealed more in workshops and literature, eventually, will meet up with the eastern Tantra. As this occurs, there will be more interest and the realization that sex is not the "dirty evil" that our religious foreskinless fathers pushed onto us. Many have been brain-washed into thinking sex is an animalistic urge that puts us in a class with jungle animals. The reality is that sex is probably the one thing pushed our evolution as humans further and faster than anything else by causing deep changes in the mind through stimulation and connecting us to our souls.

My personal experience with running energies from all the Planes, and having felt many energies from the planes, has shown me that the transformation of sexual energy to spiritual energy and using those practices, with sex takes you very high. Cosmic plane energies are powerful and plentiful for the disciplined follower of these methods. This does not imply that these are the only, or best, ways to approach or to reach the creator, but they are rewarding in their own way on a daily basis. No one spiritual system has all the answers, and no one path is right for everyone.

Mystery schools in the past have often used sex secretly as a powerful catalyst in their energy workings. Robert Anton Wilson wrote of this when researching the Illuminati and Mason factions as well as what is being learned of the secrets of spiritual energies gained from sex. Wilson has brought more to public light than most others on the subject. Magazines such as "Tantra" also offer information on techniques and list up-to-date reviews on books and classes.

Mantac Chia has several books on how to circulate, manipulate and transform energies within the body with good descriptions of these methods. Mantac has released Asian secrets hidden for centuries, previously given to the religious and ruling elite, and they are mad! Many teachers and schools throughout time have spoon-feed students while charging a FORTUNE for these hidden secrets. In olden times, a person would be hand picked, indebted forever to attend such schools, and would swear to keep these secrets of this power. For years you would study under a master and slowly you would pick up, psychically, the abilities of the teacher and their knowledge. Today you can learn many of these secrets from books, and if you have the discipline to apply them, you will advance much faster than what was allowed in the past.

For even faster results, Taoist classes are held in five centers in the U.S. and a central one in Thailand where Mantac Chia teaches with his wife. The classes and books cover several subjects that intermingle and seem very complex. Only the basic exercises are needed, and several books have those explained in a clear way. There are two on cultivating male and female sexual energies; another covers martial arts fighting and how to condense CHI for a stronger body and bones. The best book, overall, is "The Healing Tao," which contains general healing exercises and explanations. Don't be overwhelmed by the many number of exercises in these books, often just a few key ones are necessary for you to show progress.

Other classes on Tantra are oriented towards couples and range in price and are limited to certain locations. These are more geared toward enhancing their sexual relationship and are balanced with male and female class members. You can first learn about these methods from books, also the classes will mean more if you have been exposed to the concepts before investing money and travel for a workshop. References are available at the end of the chapter.

Drawing CHI into the body instead of letting it leak out as happens provides the energy to revitalize our body and mind. As with deep breathing in Yoga (Yogic breath), which charges the stack of storage cells, Tantra pumps up the internal energies and promotes health. There are methods of increasing the strength of the bones, and of wrapping CHI into the organs to bring health. This concept is like radionics bringing up the frequency of the organ to promote health.

Tantra is great for couples, it opens whole new avenues for love and intimacy. Many workshops are available to help those overcome fears about their bodies, and sex, such as the Human Awareness Institute series, "Sex, Love and Intimacy" held in some cities and also at California's Harbin Hot springs near Calistoga. Couples may experience powerful changes for the better. So have patience and make the commitment to use these methods for some time, not only a week or two, to create a strong lasting bond.

Try to offer this as a gift to the other person, such as a form of worship. Treating each other like gods / goddesses on occasion is a conscious way to show love. Don't approach this as a way to get something back. Instead give energy and if you do receive something in return it will be a wonderful reward. I have experienced wonderful feelings from giving my lover's energy, then receiving a burst of pleasant energy as well as blending our energies together and bringing them up the spine.

Much of this work and others (Such as Egyptian Mystery Schools) deals with the drawing in and accessing energies from other planets. This is used to advance faster spiritually and can be an interesting subject to learn. Get out there and try them all!!

Books:
Author, Mantac Chia and Maneewan Chia:
Taoist Secrets of Love, Cultivating the Male Sexual Energy
Healing Love Through the Tao, Cultivating the Female Sexual Energy

Awakening the Healing Light,
Fusion of the Five Elements

Kundalini Yoga for the West.　　By Sirananda Rakha, Shambhala.

Kundalini　By Ajit Mookerje

Encyclopedia of Erotic Wisdom

The Lover Within,　　By Julie Henderson

The Anatomy of Sex and Power　　By Michael Hutchison

CHAPTER TEN: TOOLS FOR THE TRADE

In the growing trade of subtle energy healing, there are more options than one can ever imagine. As a Computer Engineer / technical specialist, I know there are many powerful electrical and subtle energy widgets out there to buy and help people on their path to the God/ess within. On my path of helping myself and others, I played with many tools. At one point I felt it important to concentrate on the laying on of hands more than using implements, but of course, a different idea was presented. As soon as I had made that commitment then three people introduced me to new and exciting devices and asked for electronic healing technical help. One was a powerful item - wonderful to feel and built from electronics. Later the Reiki Master who had taught me well asked if I would build a simple electronic 555 timer circuit to "Zap the bugs" in the body. OK, OK, I'll do the electronic and widget thing again!

One thing about computers is that they show how unnecessarily afraid people become when faced with new and the unknown. You have probably seen others (like yourself) who cringe and become stressed when first they touch a computer keyboard. DO NOT BE AFRAID OF TECHNOLOGY!

It is simply an addition to our lives that will improve and streamline our efficiency. Ever since electricity was discovered it was put to work on health problems and has caused major changes to society. If you enter the hospital ward for premature infants, you will see rows of high quality electronics designed to monitor these struggling souls.

Metaphysical healing devices were scoffed at by medical professionals but are now becoming accepted by consumer markets that know they really work. So we'll review some of the electronic and static devices available today, and their sources. If Electronic healing devices are not oriented to the scientific measuring devices or methods of the day, they are often suppressed by the powers that be. Medical professions are like any other when it comes to change, it takes too much work and energy. Many keep making the same mistakes, rather than shift to a better method. Beware, as some sales businesses can be flaky , so you are on your own in dealing with them.

As with any healing modality one item may not cure all problems. Each person has a unique body chemistry with it's own end results. Be aware that testimonials are often the only selling point allowed to be used to market a product (according to the Food and Drug administration). What works for others may not work for you, so research and compare before you leap (or your money leaps from you wallet).

STATIC DEVICES:

Crystals: There is already so much information available on that so

that I will point out basics and make creative suggestions to start you out.

Energies flow from crystals that are etheric or healing in their properties.

Different materials from the earth resonate with unique frequencies, often

according to the crystal's shape and geometry which affects different parts of

a person's energies. They can be used to amplify the subtle energies that

people put out from their hands and other energy centers. (Marcel Vogel's work.)

Wear them, carry them and start a modest collection to assist in

your work. Good books are available that give the uses and characteristics of many

minerals and crystals, also retail shops and healers can make useful suggestions.

There are attunements, both for increasing your powers into the crystals and

to actually enhance the crystal's energetic strength. The attunements in the

SUN Crystal workshop can give you an extra edge in using crystals but it

is not necessary to use the crystals. The Twelve rays class provides an

energy grid attunement which increases the actual power of the crystal or

energy device, permanently.

Crystals are used by a friend in the practice of hypnotherapy with

an array of crystals that were put at different spots on and around the body to stimulate

energy bodies and produce a stronger effect. Crystals do have a tendency to

hold certain undesirable energies. They need to be cleaned, therefore they do

require some maintenance. Several methods can be used as shown in the next section.

Generators: As many are available you should try them before buying them. The feelings and effects obtained may vary considerably from other's. Results, prices vary, and are not always related to the strength or usefulness of the device. The distributors can be spread out over the world and it can be a lot to search for them.

Other countries have a greater variety, because of their acceptance and open-mindedness about these items as healing modalities. I sampled a flat soft pack from Japan to be used for healing injuries. I felt a definite soothing energy flow from it, but the price of 70 dollars (mucho yen) was a bit much! Exotic generators may cost from 200 to 500 dollars, so you must justify the expense and value to your health problems or those of your clients or customers. If something adds to your life, the cost may be nothing compared to the relief it brings.

European countries have energy devices that are commercially available, but they can not make claims about there effectiveness in the US where our laws are different. Radionics and Subtle Energy work is more recognized in Europe and Australia and is accepted, organized and more professional than in the US. For example there are laws against using radionics devices, here, for medical purposes. The same is true of the simple Orgone accumulator and other basic magnetic items. Often these laws in the US were created to protect business from competition by outlawing the devices and making them unavailable to the public. Often, big business would have their congress person write laws to "save the public" from a perceived evil, but it was often a case of protectionism for an industry such as chemical or pharmaceutical. The corruption of businesses "owning" legislative leaders has been common in politics in most countries throughout history.

Purple plate: A thin plate of metal that has been molecularly changed to reduce or remove the negative energies in crystals, food, water and also people.   The purple plate is inexpensive, simple and can be felt by many, but not all, as producing an energetic effect.   My personal experience is to call it the "purple positive attitude plate."   When I am having a bad day at work and my attitude is going downhill, I wear the smaller plate.   The change occurs later when I have a better attitude toward what was frustrating me at the time.

They can also be used in the refrigerator to reduce negative energies in food placed on the plate, and can be placed on someone while running subtle energy on them.   Some find the larger one overpowering, while others may feel it mildly.   They are available from: Tools for Exploration, San Rafael California.

Claris: This device is one of the time tested devices that reduces or eliminates the problems from electrical and electronic radiation emissions. There is enough evidence that CRTs, TVs and many consumer products are putting out harmful emissions, in many frequencies, that can damage health. If you are exposed to large amounts, as in the computer industry, then consider this small but effective device to clean up your environment, they are about $ 170.00 and have been sold for years.

Vitic Generator: This item is a hand held device that can be bought or made with simple materials.   The commercial Vitic generator from Borderland Science is a hand held item consisting of a carbon rod and a special magnetic rod for about $80 mail order. They are like a small energy pump that can constantly tap into the Prana or Mana energies and can stimulate or relax an individual with flowing energy. The rod is a carbon cutting type used by welders and can be bought from a welding supply store near you, but is not the important part of this generator. Still, you may wish to buy some of these pure carbon rods for clearing energy or holding in the hand during meditation. The other is a magnetic rod in a handle that puts out energy.

This discovery came from Egyptian royal mummies with a crook and flail in their hands and concealed in the handles were a rod of carbon (to purify) and a lodestone rod with magnet properties. It was used as a power source and is often depicted being held by royal elite in Egyptian art.

Another design (possibly from Francis Mesmer) uses a pair of horseshoe magnets and a steel rod with a Lahavoski coil mounted on a piece of wood. This design is available from Borderland Science Company P.O. Box 220, Bayside, California 95524.   Vitic generator

This design can be used creatively by putting multiple wire loops and also by hanging a birthstone crystal on the steel handle, specific for the user. This type of design needs "keeper plates" over the horseshoe magnets when not in use, so it is less convenient to use than the Borderlands model. The keeper plates are only for keeping up the strength on the magnets when not in use, and are easy to deal with. A magnetized steel dowsing rod shows a small back and forth oscillation around the Mesmer type of Vitic generator's base that is slow sweeping, like a change between Yin and Yang.

Stack Vitic: This simple design from Borderland Science Magazine is a metal tube filled with layers of granite and carbon that puts out a steady flow of Prana or Mana energy, and can be used for charging yourself up when either tired or feeling down. Like other Vitic generators, it can be used for waking up or for stimulation. An addition to the design was to run a copper tube, instead of a wire, down the center to allow air to pass through or water to charge the medium with the energies generated in the stack. Article in Borderland Science magazine.

Focusing devices: These are commercially available but do carry the warning that they are not to be used for medical purposes.   The purpose of this category is to collect or focus the energies around us or coming from the Cosmos. As an optical lens focuses light, so can cosmic and solar prana can be focused and tuned in.   We know that photons and waves can be shaped by lenses and bent to our desires and these devices have been demonstrated repeatedly to "do things".

Pyramids: Little needs to be said. Most scientists scoff at pyramid power, but the pyramids of Egypt will stand for thousands of years after the builders have passed. These monuments to metaphysical science have produced countless scientific studies and used for charging with energies from above. Most are sold in miniature form and are used for meditation enhancement or to bring in more energy from cosmic sources.   Some use crystal caps that can enhance the energies. (Mystics say the great pyramids used caps of exotic material).

Many forms of meditation pyramids are available to enhance the energies coming into you during meditation and energy work. I've used a five sided pyramid during private sessions with the SUN network to bring in energies of a particular frequency. Some use quartz crystals on the cap to focus the down flow which enters the crown of the head. A shop in Sedona Arizona makes a wonderful copper pipe pyramid that is used for meditation. Many are adding a crystal at the top of the pyramid to enhance the effect.

Orgone Accumulator: Wilhelm Reich invented this valuable tool and was punished dearly for it. The device is a simple to build box that could capture and hold atmospheric prana or life energy. It would also reflect in and hold your own personal energy if you sit inside. The effect may be a charging of the subtle bodies with prana. The boxes were rented out by Reich to reduce or slow down cancer growth. Several organizations sell them; others sell books on how to build them from inexpensive materials such as wool, wood, steel sheet or steel wool. The Orgone Accumulator Handbook, by James Demeo is a good one to start with.

Orgone blankets may be a lot more practical to own and use than a large, box accumulator type. They can be bought or made easily with instructions from the above book and using the sources listed. If you sew, then make it yourself and experiment with charging them, but follow the directions carefully as they can also accumulate negative energies.

These devices must be kept away from all negative energy emitters such as TVs, microwaves, computers, electrical motors, electric blankets, etc. Any device that can collect and accumulate positive healing energies can gather negative energies.

Biocircuits and Substance Circuits: Eeman invented these simple devices in the early 1900's to help reach particular areas of his body, his hands could not reach. To him, the key was in Christ's use of the hands to heal. He then applied these to others, using multiple people in the wire circuits for powerful healing effects. These devices have been rediscovered and are being sold in simple, as well as complex forms. The model sold by Tools for Exploration in San Raphael California, can be used by anyone for deep relaxation or to run subtle healing energies on themselves. There is a more expensive and powerful model called the Lindeman super circuit that is even better but costs much more.

All of these models can be made by anyone who can hold a soldering iron and sew a seam with instructions from the book "Biocircuits" by Terry and Linda Patten (also available at Tools for Exploration). The instructions are clear and informative and there are no electronics involved in the construction. You can save yourself money by doing it yourself with these instructions.

I love the deep relaxation obtained in 30 minutes or less. You can put a client into them and run energy in at the crown of the head and the wire circuit will flow it around blockages in the body to most areas.

A simple Biocircuit can be purchased for about $75.00, and a Super Lindeman Biocircuit for $350.00 from Tools for Exploration. You can build the Super for $100.00 or less, IF you can find the pure copper parts necessary. Copper screen can be found at some door / screen stores, so call around.

Musical Devices and Toning: There is too much information to include here but these are some of the best items available to the public.

Large Quartz Tibetan bowls are a new space age technology applied to ancient tonal mastery. They are 10 to 14 inch quartz glass bowls rubbed around the outside rim to produce continuous tones, and they have many harmonics and overtones. They can be used to vibrate the body to bring up internal frequencies much like a pipe organ in a large church (but at a lower cost than a $100,000 pipe organ). One must experience them to understand the impact. One demonstration included five bowls played by two people, and the different frequencies were sympathetically oscillating different parts of my back and body.

Heart zones music tape effects the way we interact with our heart.

-Institute of Heartmath has addressed communication between the heart and the mind. They teach classes on how to listen and talk to the heart which is what our ancestors did in a more effective way. The music industry created a termed "designer music" popular for enhancing communication with your heart, like a second mind. The music called "Heart Zones" lets you focus more on the heart and can be used with their techniques to reduce stress and acquire better health. Their scientific approach and study has proven that anger and hateful emotions cause the immune system to crash for up to 6 hours following one such incident. Their methods and tapes can reduce harmful emotions and bring the immune system back up from the previously stressed levels.

Research on the effects of the immune system were conducted under rigorous scientific conditions and are available to the public. Several workshops and also a home study program with reasonably priced books. Their music is also available at some stores or can be ordered from their California facility. Planetary Publications P.O. Box 66 , Boulder Creek, California. 95006

Prima Sounds are a new type of acoustic recording that use a potent dissonant musical sound that can vibrate and stimulate the charkas, they are available on CD or cassette from Megabrain Communications. These can evoke and stimulate the mind and body by sitting before your speakers to actually vibrate yourself while listening. They can be used with the following device for a stronger effect. School of Wisdom, 1661 Woodland Ave. Winter Park Fl. 32789, 407-645-3428

Somatron and similar devices utilize a set of speakers set into a table to play and vibrate the body with any music selected. This stimulates the cells and bones like a rock concert loud speakers and can bring forth emotions and reactions that may aid in releasing pent up stress and emotions. They run upwards from $800.00. Tools for Exploration, San Raphael, CA

ELECTRONIC DEVICES

Lahovski Multi Wave Oscillator: Another potentially hot device in the future,

also used in the past is the Multi Wave Oscillator (MWO). Invented in

France it was used in hospitals by George Lahovski for curing cancer and other aliments.

Many similar devices used electricity in the form of high voltage and low current

to stir up the ether energies. The subject would sit between two round antenna,

and the laying on of hands could be added when working with a group, to accelerate

effects. Information about the original devices was spotty until recently

the details were brought out in Borderland Science articles and books.

My personal experience was to be in the presence of one of the machines

in use but not in the main antenna streams. Still, it pulled me into the

cosmic plane of energies for brief moments, which was exhilarating because

of my sensitivity to energies. I had no physical problems and felt little physical

effect, but could see the potential for bringing up the frequencies of people who are ill.

Raising the vibrational "rates" in organs is a key to many healing modalities.

Cayce Violet Ray: Edgar Cayce was the most documented psychic

or prophet of our time. For years every word from his mouth was documented.

As a teenager Cayce was the first one who tied the eastern and western

religions together in a cohesive understanding way.

Edgar Cayce's work was documented because of the accuracy in diagnosing

and recommending treatments in herbal, medicinal and also the latest surgical

terms were described. Doctors sent many to him and the results were outstanding.

Attention was focused on him for years writing down recommendations for many illnesses.   You can rent files containing hundreds of readings for specific

diseases and the uses of various instruments that have been used for decades.

One of his devices for working with energy healing ($180.00 retail)

is the Violet Ray device available from Tools for Exploration or A.R.E.

It was a high voltage item that glowed with a purple plasma like energy

at the head of the device, it was used to stimulate healing properties in a

problem area of the body.   More information on it's use is available from

Association for Research and Enlightenment, in   Virginia.

One theory on high voltage items is that the voltage breaks

open the ether barrier. Another is that high voltage pulsing pushes

out vital energies and negative energies.   This is followed by an insuring

flow of life energy when the oscillator cycles down.   The other theory

which follows other modalities, is that the high voltage pulses or

waves carry multiple frequency components and bring the body's

vibrational rates up to where they should be.   Book: Vibrational

Medicine.   Cayce also had a device called the "wet cell" and a Bio energy

device for working with life energy in the body for healing. I have been

told that the violet ray device and other static devices drive entities out of the body.

Sound and Light Machines: Buddha In a can!! Wow, we can buy meditation

in a can! This new class of device is used to increase the depth of mental

states from simple meditation to an increase of channeling abilities of mediums to bring in information. These are a small box that puts out tones and light into the eyes and has an amazing ability to bring brain waves down to more relaxed alpha and theta states. Small, portable and with great variation of programs to run for different purposes these are a new revolution for the mind's evolution. More of a mind stimulation device to induce meditative states, sound and light machines are good for deep relaxation.

Several manufacturers have prices from $150.00 and up, so research the selection and try them out before purchasing. They are described well by Michael Hutchison in several books such as "Megabrain," which shows theoretical and practical uses. They are getting a strong following from the publication, Megabrain Journal, available from Tools for Exploration San Rafael, CA.

I have combined sound and light with the Lindeman Super Biocircuit, and a tape player equipped with meditation tapes or music, with tremendous results both in states of mind and deep relaxation. Meditation is a discipline that many find difficult to pursue as it may take weeks to become good at entering the meditative state on a daily basis. This is a good device for those who don't have discipline. In daily life, I prefer to meditate using traditional methods, however sound and light machines can work for other things as well.

Claims abound that deal with increasing our intelligence and opening up new pathways in the mind. This is something you may or may not experience. Personally, I am a firm believer in these devices for both enhancing the brain and opening new pathways within the mind. The device can be used for synching yourself up with the Earth resonance and to bring subjects into deep theta states, ones that help release stored traumas.

Makes and models vary in their features, and the number of programs for the dollars spent so do compare before buying. One manufacturer's newest model has the ability to plug in modules for future programs, Therefore it is very versatile and adaptable to the future market (less obsolesce due to technology changes!)
Another supplies a "card" that goes into a computer so you can create your own programs with easy-to-use software customized for you / your clients. ($500 plus your computer)

Lucid Dream Machines: This new technology is helping people achieve the mind state where one becomes more conscious during dreams and can, therefore, direct and interact with the subconscious. More devices keep being brought out and you have to search the Internet to keep abreast, so contact the retailers and manufacturers for their basic information. They vary in form and function but they generally sense when you are in the REM (dream state) during sleep and trigger something such as lights in the eyes or a tape of a voice (such as your own). This tape instructs you to be conscious of being in the dream thus you train yourself to become active during that state. For more information see the book Lucid Dreaming

How are they used together ?? First rule, "there are no rules". Use your imagination. I had profound experiences combining the Lindeman Super Biocircuit with an earth ground attachment and a sound and light machine with a chakra meditation tape played through the sound and light machine.   Repeated use of this combination brought me to states of mind I had only heard of before. In using the combination twice a week for one year I stumbled onto the Shamadi states that can take years to achieve.   You may have a different reaction together.

The only problem with some of the energy devices is that they are strong enough to "overcharge" your subtle bodies and mind with more energy than can be used at one time, therefore they will cause mild anxiety or irritation. Unlike the intelligent energy systems that turn off when you've had enough,   these devices keep pumping out their power although you are filled with Prana or Mana. There are simple ways to avoid this by limiting your time on the device such as: 30 minutes on a biocircuit or 10 minutes on a Vitic generator.

Most of these devices will enhance the laying on of hands and can be used on clients with interesting results. I loaned a purple plate to a person who said when they slept on it, their insomnia disappeared. For myself, the purple plate is so powerful I can't sleep with one in the bedroom. Having someone hold a purple plate tells more than anything else.   Interactions with their energy fields may produce colors, swirling or feelings emerging.

Put someone on a biocircuit for 30 minutes either before a massage or while doing Subtle energy laying on of hands in order to relax them more deeply. When running energies on yourself, you can use a sound and light machine set for the Schuman resonance or 7.8 to 8 hertz, to link up to the earth's natural resonance. It is common for healers to sync up to the earth both resonantly and energetically through the process of grounding.

Sound and light machines programmed for bringing the mind to a theta brain wave state may be good for hypnotherapy also for running energy to induce hypnotic suggestions or approach childhood memories. Such memories are often recalled in a slower mental brain wave state, where they are stored away. The Hawaiians used a combination of hypnotherapy and laying on of hands. When the practitioner gave a "post hypnotic suggestion," such as to stop smoking or change a behavior they would induce "Mana" with the laying on of hands to make it stick in the mind. Including a sound and light machine in the theta state setting may help this process even more.

You can break through limits much faster using this technology our ancestors did not. The modern world has given us many complex appliances to assist our lives. As a healer you can pick and choose from simple, inexpensive tools to costly, far reaching and mind expanding wizard boxes. Unchain your mind and let it loose in the candy store of life, but most of all, have FUN!! Yahoo!!!

The SPIRITUAL UNFOLDMENT NETWORK (SUN) is a non-denominational spiritually oriented network of teachers dedicated to making available to the general public esoteric energy work from all major spiritual traditions. SUN's goal is to assist people in progressing more effectively on their personal and spiritual growth. Done without personality worship or dictating the path. We provide tools and attunements for spiritual advancement.

Teaching the latest technologies of Subtle Energy systems of major spiritual traditions from around the world. Many spiritually and healing oriented students from all over the country and world with varied backgrounds brings much esoteric knowledge to share. Keith lectures, writes and conducts classes in powerful systems from many cultures to help those on a path.

Keith has achieved the third level of teacher attunements with access to many lineages of teachings. By using the systems from all over the world you can choose the right one for you, that will benefit you the most and help you your true self and connect with your divine guides and helpers.

Esoteric energy systems can accelerate spiritual advancement and have been used by many cultures from around the world. We do not dictate the path, only you do that Many systems from all over the world are taught and practiced by Keith, some of them are:

-Reiki -Third degree master. (Japanese origin) Teacher: Jeanine Sande

-Huna (Hawaiian) There are seven levels. Huna is heart oriented and grounding.

-Drisana (Tibetan origin) The most versatile and sophisticated of the SUN teachings.

-Twelve Rays - An Enhancement to all energy systems from all schools.

-Egyptian - Green energy, Bliss of Osiris, Nectar of the Sphinx, Phoenix Rising.

-Egyptian Mystery school student under Irving Feurst. This is a very extensive system.

-Neriya - Accelerates spiritual evolution more than other systems.

-Angel energy - Angel energies and classes connect you with the internet of the Angels.

-Hindu - Gayatri (mantra meditation), Kundalini water

-Certified Massage Practitioner (Swedish and Watsu) Accupressure certified.

Keith Darwin Rector teaches (since 1994) these subtle energy systems in western style Workshops with manuals describing each attunement and how to use them.
An author of Two books:
"Jack of All Subtle Energies" a book on the many energy systems from all over the world.
"Life Energy LIVES AGAIN" a book on scientists that used the subtle energies.

Self realization modalities accessed for spiritual advancement and subtle energy channeling:
Amanae (5 and 2 day participant) Tai Chi, Taoist practices (Mantac Chia's teaching)
Bio Circuit work (Supercircuit) Sound and Light Machines, Large Tibetan bowls.
Yoga practice, Human Awareness Institute workshops 1-4.
Polynesian Dancer, Hula, Tahitian, Drumming and singer.

Keith Darwin Rector   Email: **darwin@cruzio.com**

www.spiritunfoldment .ORG